New Edition

Viewfinder

Topics

Britain in Europe

Conflict, Peace, Partnership

compiled and edited
by
David Beal

Langenscheidt

Berlin · München · Wien · Zürich · New York

Viewfinder

Topics

Unterrichtsmaterialien für die Sekundarstufe II

Britain in Europe

Conflict, Peace, Partnership

Herausgeber:
Prof. em. Dr. Dr. h.c. mult. Peter Freese, Paderborn

Autor:
David Beal

Projekt-Team:
Dr. Martin Arndt, Münster
Prof. Dr. Mita Banerjee, Siegen
David Beal, M. A., Bochum
Cornelia Becker, Bremen
Dr. Peter Dines, Cert. Ed., Ludwigsburg
Prof. i. R. Dr. Hanspeter Dörfel, Ludwigsburg
OStR Dieter Düwel, Castrop-Rauxel
Prof. em. Dr. Dr. h.c. Dr. h. c. Peter Freese, Paderborn
Dr. Carin Freywald †
Jennifer von der Grün, B. A., Dortmund
OStR Ulrich Imig, Wildhausen
OStR Reimer Jansen, Oyten-Sagehorn
Dr. Michael Mitchell, M. A., Reken und Warwick
Prof. Dr. Michael Porsche, Paderborn
StD i. E. Detlef Rediker, Lippstadt
StD Dr. Peter-J. Rekowski, Kirchhain
StD i.K. Peter Ringeisen, M. A., Amberg
Karl Sassenberg, Münster
StD Henning Scholz †
StD Dr. Annegret Schrick, Essen
OStR Ekkehard Sprenger, Kiel
StR Susanne Stadler, Wiesbaden
OStD Dr. Dietrich Theißen †
Donald Turner, M. A. †
Prof. Dr. Laurenz Volkmann, Jena
Philip Wade, M. A., Cert. Ed., Amberg

Verlagsredaktion: Dr. Beatrix Finke
Visuelles Konzept: Barbara Slowik, Atelier S., München
Layout und Produktion: kaltnermedia GmbH, Bobingen

www.langenscheidt.de/viewfinder

Umwelthinweis: Gedruckt auf chlorfrei gebleichtem Papier.

1. Auflage 2008

© 2008 Langenscheidt ELT GmbH, München

Das Werk und seine Teile sind urheberrechtlich geschützt. Jede Verwertung in anderen als den gesetzlich zugelassenen Fällen bedarf deshalb der vorherigen schriftlichen Einwilligung des Verlages.

Printed in Germany
ISBN 978-3-526-51062-8

Contents

Britain in Europe .... p. 4

1 | **David Beal: What is Britain?** .... p. 6
　　　Info: A brief chronology of Britain .... p. 8

2 | **Norman Davies: What is Europe?*** .... p. 9
　　　Info: The boundaries of Europe .... p. 12

3 | **David Beal: The Growth of National Stereotypes** .... p. 13

4 | **George Mikes: *How to be an Alien*** .... p. 16

5 | **Sir Owen Seaman: "The Englishman on the French Stage"** ..... p. 19

6 | **Stephen Clarke: An Englishman in Paris*** .... p. 21
　　　Info: "Ministère de la Francophonie" .... p. 23

7 | **Robert Southey: "After Blenheim"** .... p. 25
　　　Info: The Battle of Blenheim .... p. 27
　　　Background Reading: Battles in European History .... p. 27

8 | **Len Deighton: *SS-GB*** .... p. 28

9 | **Bert Trautmann – the German who became an Englishman*** .. p. 31

10 | **John King: The Football Hooligan** .... p. 33

11 | **"We want to be loved by you…"** .... p. 35

12 | **1946 – Winston Churchill calls for a United States of Europe*** . p. 39

13 | **Timothy Garton Ash: Janus Britain*** .... p. 42

14 | **Norman Davies: Britain and Europe get closer together*** ..... p. 45
　　　Info: Alternative history – fiction and non-fiction .... p. 47

15 | **Malcolm Bradbury: Broken English*** .... p. 48
　　　Info: "You can say you to me" .... p. 51

16 | **Jonathan Lynn and Antony Jay: Party Games – Using Europe in British Politics*** ... p. 51
　　　Info: The main characters in this episode of *Yes, Prime Minister* ... p. 54

17 | **T. R. Reid: Steve Thoburn – the Metric Martyr*** .... p. 56

18 | **Henry Porter: What we want from Europe** .... p. 58

19 | **Britain: A Magnet for Migrants*** .... p. 60

20 | **Nicholas Fraser: How to be a European** .... p. 62

* Titles provided by the editor

Britain in Europe

IDEAS

SPORTS

PEOPLE

ART AND LITERATURE

What do you know about Britain?
- What is the official name of Britain?
- Who gave Britain its name?
- What part of Britain is "Great" Britain?
- Which are the four national soccer teams that represent Britain?

What has Europe given to Britain?
What has Britain given to Europe?

INVENTIONS

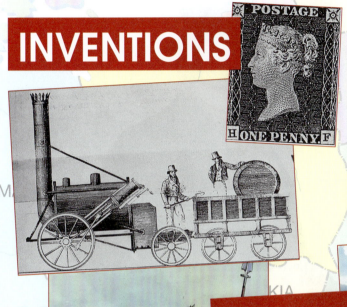

FOOD AND DRINK

FASHION

What do you know about Europe?
- Where did Europe get its name?
- Which is the most densely populated European country?
- Which is the second largest European country after Russia?
- Where was the treaty signed that started the European Union?
- Which two countries have rejected membership of the European Union?
- Name the two European countries which each consist of one whole island.
- Which is the smallest European country?
- In which country is the geographical centre of Europe situated?

1 David Beal

What is Britain?

The task of defining Britain is more complex than might seem at first glance. "Britain" can, like "Ireland", be used both as a political and a geographical term and in both areas, politics and geography, it can be used with a variety of meanings.

1 "Britain", by far the most commonly used name for the country whose official name is "The United Kingdom of Great Britain and Northern Ireland",
5 has no official status. It doesn't appear on official name plates at international conferences, it's not used on car nationality plates, and it's not on the British passport. But it does appear in
10 the titles of many books and publications dealing with Britain: *Britain: A Handbook* (London: Central Office of Information, 2007), *Reader's Digest Illustrated Encyclopedia of Britain*, ed.
15 Justin Scott-McNab (London: Reader's Digest, 1999), David Gentleman, *David Gentleman's Britain* (London: Weidenfeld and Nicholson, 1982), Anthony Sampson, *Who Runs This*
20 *Place? The Anatomy of Britain in the 21st Century* (London: John Murray, 2005), David Dimbleby (ed.), *A Picture of Britain* (London: Tate Publishing, 2004) and indeed in the
25 Viewfinder series: *Politics in Britain, Education in Britain and the USA*, and *Minorities in Britain*.

If we look again at the official name for Britain, "The United Kingdom of
30 Great Britain and Northern Ireland", we are confronted with the problem of the term "Great Britain". The official name indicates that the UK is made up of two distinct geographical areas: the
35 largest island in the archipelago usually known as the British Isles, "Great Britain", and "Northern Ireland", the northern part of another island called Ireland. So "Great Britain" is a geo-
40 graphical term. Possibly.

Unfortunately "Great Britain" is also used, mainly but not only, by Americans to refer to "Britain", as when President George W. Bush
45 greeted Tony Blair in Washington as "The Prime Minister of Great Britain". This may just be common

John Bull, created by Dr John Arbuthnot in 1712, is a national personification of Britain

American usage, or a mistaken belief that "Great" Britain is a more complimentary name than just "Britain".

In many European languages, too, translations of "Great Britain" seem to be the usual title for the country officially known as the "United Kingdom (of Great Britain and Northern Ireland)". If we look up "Britain" in large bilingual dictionaries, we get the following results: in German (*Langenscheidt Großwörterbuch Englisch,* München: Langenscheidt, 2004) *Großbritannien,* in French (*The Oxford-Hachette French Dictionary,* Oxford: Oxford University Press, 2001) *Grande Bretagne,* in Spanish (*The Oxford Spanish Dictionary,* Oxford: Oxford University Press, 1998) *Gran Bretaña,* and in Italian (*The Collins Italian Dictionary,* Glasgow: HarperCollins, 2005) *Gran Bretagna.* Confusion between a geographical entity, the island of Great Britain, and a political entity, Britain or the United Kingdom, is therefore widespread. The confusion is increased when we consider that the British nationality plate for cars is GB. This clearly refers to the political unit, United Kingdom, since cars from Northern Ireland also use GB. A more logical nationality code would have been UK. An additional anomaly is that in international currency trading the British currency, the pound sterling, is referred to not as UKP, but as GBP. When Internet domain names were being allocated in the 1990s, many British government departments adopted the code <gov.gb> and only changed to <gov.uk> at a second attempt (Norman Davies, *The Isles: A History,* London: Macmillan, 1999, p. xxxix).

A further problem is that both within and outside Britain there is widespread confusion between the terms "England" and "Britain". For many people, the terms are thought, wrongly, to be synonyms. This can cause a complete breakdown in understanding as in Vernon Coleman's book *England Our England: A Nation in Jeopardy* (Barnstaple: Blue Books, 2003), since we are never sure whether he is writing about England or Britain. In many European languages, in fact, the word for "England", *Angleterre* (Fr.), *Inglaterra* (Sp.) and *Inghilterra* (It.) is the commonly used word for "Britain". And from looking at German documents in both world wars one might easily have thought that these were wars between Germany and England and not Britain. Some writers try to have it both ways. Hans-Dieter Gelfert entitled his book about Britain – or is it really about England? *Typisch englisch: Wie die Briten wurden, wie sie sind* (München: Verlag C. H. Beck, 1995). However, citizens of the United Kingdom, although all British by nationality, tend to identify themselves first and foremost with the nation of Britain they come from: England, Wales, or Scotland. In Northern Ireland the situation is more complicated and people there may call themselves Irish, British, Ulstermen or -women, or even Scottish, depending on their religion or political affiliation.

History adds a further complicating dimension which can confuse even the most knowledgeable writer. In *The Sunday Times* of 26 July 1998 Sir Francis Drake, English seaman, privateer and pirate, who sailed round the world from 1577–81 and fought against the Spanish Armada in 1588, was described to the horror of many of that paper's English readers as "That quintessentially British gentleman-adventurer ...". More unfortunately, in the introduction to *The Oxford Illustrated History of Britain* (Kenneth O. Morgan (ed.), Oxford: Oxford University Press, 1986) the editor writes about Venetian ambassadors meeting the British and dealing with "British society" in the late fifteenth century. "Britain", however, did not come into existence until the union of England and Scotland in 1707. This created for the very first time the political entity known as the United Kingdom, with citizens who slowly learned to call themselves British as well as English, Welsh or Scottish.

Vocabulary

8 nationality plate (n.): sign on a car showing which country it comes from – **49 complimentary** (adj.): saying that you admire s.th. or s.o. – **64 entity** (n.): s.th. that exists as a single and complete unit – **72 anomaly** (n.): s.th. that is noticeable because it is different from what is usual – **73 currency** (n.): the type of money that a country uses – **75 domain name** (n.): the first part of a website's address, which usually begins with "www." – **75 to allocate** (v.): give s.th. to s.o. esp. after an official decision has been made – **105 affiliation** (n.): connection that s.o. has with a political, religious etc. organisation – **113 quintessentially** (adv.): being a perfect example of a particular type of person or thing – **117 Venetian** (adj.): /vəˌniːʃən/ coming from the city of Venice in Italy – **117 ambassador** (n.): an important official who represents their government in a foreign country

Explanations

44 George W. Bush: (b. 1946) forty-third president of the USA, elected in 2000, re-elected in 2004 – **45 Tony Blair:** (b. 1953) British Labour politician, prime minister from 1997 to 2007; full name Anthony Charles Lynton Blair. – **108 The Sunday Times:** largest-selling British quality Sunday newspaper – **108 Sir Francis Drake:** (c. 1540–96), English sailor and explorer. He was the first Englishman to circumnavigate the globe (1577–80). He played an important part in the defeat of the Spanish Armada. – **111 Spanish Armada:** a Spanish naval invasion force sent against England in 1588 by Philip II of Spain.

AWARENESS

1 Write brief definitions of the following terms: a) Britain b) Great Britain c) England d) United Kingdom e) Ireland. Make clear the distinction between the political and the geographical meanings of the words.

COMPREHENSION

2 Explain why the Internet name gov.gb for British government departments was not a good idea.
3 Explain why the book title *Typisch englisch: Wie die Briten wurden, wie sie sind* (ll. 96f.) could be considered rather strange.
4 Why was Sir Francis Drake not a "British gentleman-adventurer" (l. 113) and why did the Venetian ambassadors not meet any "British" people (l. 118)?
5 Why is "England" used to refer to "Britain" so frequently?

PROJECT

6 Investigate the use of and meanings given for "Britain" and "Great Britain" in dictionaries, guides on English usage, and encyclopedias.

A brief chronology of Britain

1189–72	English conquest of Ireland begins
1277–84	English conquest of Wales
1536–42	Acts of Union integrate England and Scotland
1603	The Plantation of Ulster: Scots and English Protestant settlers move into Northern Ireland – they are the first true "British" people.
1707	Act of Union unites England and Scotland to form the United Kingdom of Great Britain
1801	Act of Union unites Great Britain and Ireland to form the United Kingdom of Great Britain and Ireland (1707–1800). This is the only period in which the United Kingdom shares exactly the same territory as Great Britain.
1921	Ireland is partitioned. The Irish Free State, later the Republic of Ireland (Eire), becomes an independent state. The six counties in the north of Ireland, Northern Ireland, remain part of the United Kingdom, now renamed the United Kingdom of Great Britain and Northern Ireland.

These flags represent Scotland (top left), Wales (top right), Northern Ireland (bottom left) and England (bottom right)

2 What is Europe?*

Norman Davies

The answer to this question might seem fairly obvious, but as Norman Davies shows here, defining what Europe is can be a rather complicated matter. In this extract he discusses the cultural and political roots of Europe and the difficulties of setting the geographical limits of the continent. – Norman Davies, *Europe: A History* (Oxford: Oxford University Press, 1986), pp. 7–10.

'Europe' is a relatively modern idea. It gradually replaced the earlier concept of 'Christendom' in a complex intellectual process lasting from the fourteenth to the eighteenth centuries. The decisive period, however, was reached in the decades either side of 1700 after generations of religious conflict. In that early phase of the Enlightenment it became an embarrassment for the divided community of nations to be reminded of their common Christian identity; and 'Europe' filled the need for a designation with more neutral connotations. In the West, the wars against Louis XIV inspired a number of publicists who appealed for common action to settle the divisions of the day. The much imprisoned Quaker William Penn (1644–1718), son of an Anglo-Dutch marriage and founder of Pennsylvania, had the distinction of advocating both universal toleration and a European parliament. The dissident French abbé, Charles Castel de St Pierre (1658–1743), author of *Projet d'une paix perpetuelle* (1713), called for a confederation of European powers to guarantee a lasting peace. In the East, the emergence of the Russian Empire under Peter the Great required radical rethinking of the international framework. The Treaty of Utrecht of 1713 provided the last major occasion when public reference to the Respublica Christiana, the 'Christian Commonwealth' was made.

After that, the awareness of a European as opposed to a Christian community gained the upper hand. Writing in 1751, Voltaire described Europe as:

'a kind of great republic divided into several states, some monarchical, the others mixed ... but all corresponding with one another. They all have the same religious foundation, even if divided into several confessions. They all have the same principle of public law and politics, unknown in other parts of the world.'

"Queen Europe" – an engraving from an edition of Sebastian Müntzer's (also Münster's) *Cosmography* (1544)

Twenty years later, Rousseau announced: 'There are no longer Frenchmen, Germans, and Spaniards, or even English, but only Europeans.' According to one judgement, the final realization of the 'idea of Europe' took place in 1796, when Edmund Burke wrote: 'No European can be a complete exile in any part of Europe.' Even so, the geographical, cultural and political parameters of the European community have always remained open to debate. In 1794, when William Blake published one of his most unintelligible poems entitled 'Europe: A Prophecy', he illustrated it with a picture of the Almighty leaning out of the heavens and holding a pair of compasses.

Most of Europe's outline is determined by its extensive sea-coasts. But the delineation of its land frontier was long in the making. The dividing line between Europe and Asia had been fixed by the ancients from the Hellespont to the River Don, and it was still there in medieval times. A fourteenth-century encyclopedist could produce a fairly precise definition:

'Europe is said to be a third of the whole world, and has its name from Europa, daughter of Agenor, King of Libya. Jupiter ravished this Europa, and brought her to Crete, and called most of the land after her Europa ... Europe begins on the river Tanay [Don] and stretches along the Northern Ocean to the end of Spain. The east and south part rises from the sea called Pontus [Black Sea] and is all joined to the Great Sea [the Mediterranean] and ends at the islands of Cadiz [Gibraltar] ...'

[...]

Neither the ancients nor the medievals had any close knowledge of the easterly reaches of the European Plain, several sections of which were not permanently settled until the eighteenth century.

So it was not until 1730 that a Swedish officer in the Russian service called Strahlenberg suggested that Europe's boundary should be pushed back from the Don to the Ural mountains and the Ural River. Sometime in the late eighteenth century, the Russian government erected a boundary post on the trail between Yekatarinburg and Tyúmen to mark the frontier of Europe and Asia. From then on the gangs of Russian exiles, who were marched to Siberia in irons, created the custom of kneeling by the post and of scooping up a last handful of European earth. [...]

Geographical Europe has had to compete with notions of Europe as a cultural community; and in the absence of common political structures, European civilization could only be defined by cultural criteria. Special emphasis is usually placed on the seminal role of Christianity, a role which did not cease when the label of Christendom was dropped.

Broadcasting to a defeated Germany in 1945, the poet T. S. Eliot expounded the view that European civilization stands in mortal peril after repeated dilutions of the Christian core. He described 'the closing of Europe's mental frontiers' that had occurred during the years which had seen the nation-states assert themselves to the full. 'A kind of cultural autarchy followed inevitably on political and economic autarchy,' he said. He stressed the organic nature of culture: 'Culture is something that must grow. You cannot build a tree; you can only plant it, and care for it, and wait for it to mature ...' He stressed the interdependence of the numerous sub-cultures within the European family. What he called cultural 'trade' was the organism's lifeblood. And he stressed the centrality of the Christian tradition, which subsumes within itself 'the legacy of Greece, of Rome, and of Israel' [...]

This concept is, in all senses, the traditional one. It is the yardstick of all other variants, breakaways, and other bright ideas on the subject. It is the starting point of what Mme de Staël once called *'penser á l'européenne'*.

For cultural historians of Europe, the most fundamental of tasks is to identify the many competing strands within the Christian tradition and to gauge their weight in relation to various non-Christian and anti-Christian elements. Pluralism is de rigueur. Despite the apparent supremacy of Christian belief right up to the

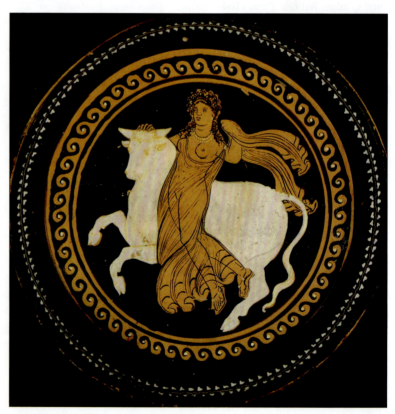

According to Greek mythology, the Phoenician princess Europa was carried off from her homeland to Crete by Zeus, the lord of the gods, in the form of a bull

mid-twentieth century, it is impossible to deny that many of the most fruitful stimuli of modern times, from the Renaissance passion for antiquity to the Romantics' obsession with Nature, were essentially pagan in character. Similarly, it is hard to argue that the contemporary cults of modernism, eroticism, economics, sport, or pop culture have much to do with the Christian heritage. The main problem nowadays is to decide whether the centrifugal forces of the twentieth century have reduced that heritage to a meaningless jumble or not. Few analysts would now maintain that anything resembling a European cultural monolith has ever existed. One interesting solution is to see Europe's cultural legacy as composed of four or five overlapping and interlocking circles. According to the novelist Alberto Moravia, Europe's unique cultural identity is 'a reversible fabric, one side variegated … the other a single colour rich and deep'.

Vocabulary

9f. embarrassment (n.): a feeling you get when you are nervous or uncomfortable because you have made a silly mistake - **13 designation** (n.): a name or title - **14 connotation** (n.): an idea that a word makes you think of that is more than its basic meaning - **15 publicist** (n.): here: a journalist; s.o. who writes about current affairs - **21 to advocate** (v.): to publicly support an idea - **23 abbé** (n.) (fr.): a French priest - **27 emergence** (n.): when s.th. begins to be known or noticed - **30 framework** (n.): the structure of a society; a legal or political system - **39 republic** (n.): here: political structure - **41 to correspond** (v.): here: communicate - **43 foundation** (n.): a basic idea, principle - **60 delineation** (n.): making the borders between two areas very clear - **77 reaches** (n.): the parts of a place that are furthest from the centre - **93 irons** (n.): /ˈaɪən/ a chain used to prevent a prisoner from moving - **94 to scoop** (v.): to pick s.th. up using your curved hand - **98 notion** (n.): idea - **104 seminal** (adj.): very important; influencing the way things develop in the future - **108 to expound** (v.): to explain or talk about s.th. in detail - **109 mortal** (adj.): extreme - **109 peril** (n.): danger - **109 dilution** (n.): making s.th. weaker or less effective - **112 to assert o.s.** (v.): here: to become strong and influential - **114 autarchy** (n.): here: independence - **117 to mature** (v.): to become fully grown or developed - **121 to subsume** (v.): to include s.th. as a member of a group - **122 legacy** (n.): s.th. that exists as a result of things that happened in the past - **125 yardstick** (n.): s.th. that you compare another thing with - **125 breakaway** (n.): change from the usual way of doing s.th. - **130 strand** (n.): one of the parts of an idea - **130 to gauge** (v.): to judge or measure - **137 obsession** (n.): an extreme unhealthy interest in s.th. - **138 pagan** (adj.): not belonging to any of the main religions of the world - **139 contemporary** (adj.): belonging to the present time - **141 heritage** (n.): the traditional beliefs and values of a society - **144 jumble** (n.): a lot of different thing mixed together - **146 monolith** (n.): a large uniform structure - **148 interlocking** (adj.): fitting together - **150 reversible** (adj.): which can be worn with either side showing on the outside - **150 fabric** (n.): cloth used for making clothes - **150 variegated** (adj.): here: with a lot of different colours and patterns

Explanations

3 Christendom: here: the Christian nations and states which owed allegiance to the Pope - **9 Enlightenment:** a set of ideas, theories and attitudes which arose and spread through Europe from the middle of the 17th century to the end of the 18th which stressed the ideas of rationalism and freedom and denied the traditional authority of monarchs and religion. - **15 Louis XIV** (1638-1715): reigned 1643-1715, known as the Sun King (*le roi soleil*). His almost constant wars of expansion united Europe against him (see Text 7 "After Blenheim") - **18 Quaker:** a member of the Religious Society of Friends, a Christian movement devoted to peaceful principles. - **18 William Penn** (1644-1718): English Quaker, founder of the state of Pennsylvania. - **23 Charles Castel de St Pierre** (1658-1743): French social philosopher and reformer who advocated a fair tax system, including a graduated income tax; he thought the state should provide free education for women as well as men. - **24f. Projet d'une paix perpetuelle:** project for a perpetual peace; written in 1713, described plans for an international court and league of states. - **25f. confederation:** an association of sovereign and independent states acting together to achieve common aims - **28 Russian Empire:** (1712-1917) founded by Peter the Great and which lasted until the Russian Revolution - **28f. Peter the Great** (1682-1725): he modernised the Russian armed forces and expanded Russian territory to the Baltic Sea. The city of St Petersburg is named after him. - **30 Treaty of Utrecht** (1713): Treaties between Britain and France on the one hand, Spain on the other, concluded British involvement in the War of the Spanish Succession. The treaty was the first major international treaty to be composed in French rather than in Latin, and invoked the concept of Balance of Power. - **33 *Respublicana Christiana*** (Lat.): Christian Commonwealth; the Christian community of European nations - **38 Voltaire** (1694-1778): French writer, dramatist, poet and Anglophile; pseudonym of Francois-Marie Arouet. He was a leading figure of the Enlightenment. - **47 Rousseau:** Jean-Jacques (1712-78) French philosopher and writer, born in Switzerland. He believed that civilisation warps the fundamental goodness of human nature. - **51 Edmund Burke** (1729-97): British statesman, philosopher and political theorist, born in Ireland - **55 William Blake** (1757-1827): English artist and poet. His poems mark the beginning of Romanticism. - **62 the ancients:** the people of ancient times, esp. the Greeks and Romans of classical antiquity - **63 Hellespont:** the ancient name for the Dardanelles - **68 Libya:** in the ancient world all of North Africa west of Egypt, now a state in North Africa - **68 Jupiter:** Roman name for the Greek god Zeus - **71 Northern Ocean:** now called the

North Sea – **72 Pontus:** here: the Black Sea – **73 the Great Sea:** the Mediterranean Sea – **74 Cadiz:** here: Gibraltar; now a city in south west Spain – **76 the medievals:** people who lived in the Middle Ages c.1000 to 1453 – **82 Strahlenberg:** Philip Johan von Strahlenberg (1646-1747); carried out research into Siberia and published it in a book which aroused great interest and was translated into English, French and Spanish. In the book he laid down a new boundary between Europe and Asia, along the Ural Mountains. – **89 Yekatarinburg:** also Ekatarinburg, an industrial city in central Russia – **89 Tyúmen:** a city in west Siberian Russia in the eastern foothills of the Ural mountains – **108 T. S. Eliot** (1888-1965): Thomas Stearns Eliot; American-born British poet and critic. He gained the Nobel Prize for literature in 1948. – **127 Mme de Staël** (1766-1817): born Anne Louise Germaine Necker; French novelist and critic – **127** *penser à l'européenne* (fr.): to think in a European manner – **132 pluralism:** system in which many ideas co-exist – **132** *de rigueur* (fr.): considered to be necessary – **136 Renaissance:** the revival of art and literature under the influence of classical models in the 14th – 16th centuries – **137 Romantics:** supporters of Romanticism, a movement in the arts and literature in the late 18th century which emphasised inspiration, subjectivity, and the importance of the individual – **139 modernism:** a movement in the arts that aims to break with classical and traditional forms – **149 Alberto Moravia:** (1907-90) one of the leading Italian novelists of the 20th century

AWARENESS

1 Define what Europe means to you. Bear in mind its geographical, historical and cultural meanings.

COMPREHENSION

2 In a chronology summarise the important moments in the movement towards a European identity mentioned in this extract.
3 What does Norman Davies mean when he writes that "Geographical Europe has had to compete with notions of Europe as a cultural community." (ll. 97 ff.)? How far is this still true today?
4 What did T. S. Eliot mean when he wrote that "Culture is something that must grow." (ll. 115 f.)?
5 What do you think are the "centrifugal forces of the twentieth century" to which Norman Davies refers?

ANALYSIS

6 How does Voltaire's statement of 1751 justify Norman Davies' contention that Europe became more than just a "Christian community" (l. 36)?
7 Explain the images used by Alberto Moravia to describe Europe's cultural identity.

PROJECTS

8 Find out more about William Penn's proposals for a European parliament.
9 Investigate the importance of the Treaty of Utrecht as a turning point in European history.
10 Investigate and write a report on the main Christian and non-Christian elements in European culture.

The boundaries of Europe

– If Turkey became a member of the European Union, "Europe" would extend into the Middle East and have borders with Iran, Iraq and Syria.
– The Eurovision song contest – sponsored by the European Broadcasting Union with Algeria, Egypt, Israel, Jordan, Morocco, Libya, and Tunisia among its members – includes Israel as a regular participant.
– Greenland – in the western North Atlantic, much nearer to Canada than to Europe – was a member of the European Union from 1973 to 1984.

Britain in Europe

3 The Growth of National Stereotypes

David Beal

The extracts below and the cartoon on p. 15 show that images we have of ourselves and others have both a long history and reach back into our childhood. It is no wonder we find it difficult to look at ourselves and others objectively.

War, the ultimate confrontation with the other, sharpens our perceptions of who we are and who our enemies are. And it was through wars with its neighbours in the British Isles – Scots, Welsh and Irish – and on the European continent – mainly the French – in the Middle Ages that the English gained awareness of themselves and others as nations. As early as 1373 an observer commented on the self-confidence of the English, derived from their successes in wars with France, saying that: 'the English are so filled with their own greatness and have won so many big victories that they have come to believe they cannot lose. In battle, they are the most confident nation in the world.' (Kenneth Morgan (ed.), *The Oxford Illustrated History of Britain,* Oxford: Oxford University Press, 1984, pp. 221f.)

By the mid-1430s the separateness of England came, in a recurring image, to be identified with its encircling seas, when a pamphleteer wrote:

Keep then the seas about in special;
Which of England is the round wall,
As though England were likened to a city
And the wall environ were the sea ... (Ibid., p. 221)

Around 1500 an Italian visitor reported that: 'the English are great lovers of themselves and of everything belonging to them. They think that there are no other men than themselves, and no other world than England; and when they see a handsome foreigner they say that "he looks like an Englishman", and that "it is a great pity that he should not be an Englishman".'

The warlike note in English national pride continued in Polydore Vergil's *Anglicae Historia* of 1534, where we read:

Come the three corners of the world in arms,
And we shall shock them. Naught shall make us rue
If England to itself do rest but true.
(Norman Davies, *The Isles: A History,* London: Macmillan, 1999, p. 385)

The same lines recur at the end of Shakespeare's *King John*, when Philip Falconbridge, the bastard son of King Richard I, declares:

This England never did, nor never shall,
Lie at the proud foot of a conqueror,
But when it first did help to wound itself.
Now these her princes are come home again,
Come the three corners of the world in arms,
And we shall shock them. Naught shall make us rue
If England to itself do rest but true.
(*King John,* Act V, Scene VII)

Shakespeare, writing both for the mass of the people and the political establishment, was, in his historical dramas, telling how 'Tudor England, having turned its back on medieval blood and strife, had entered an era of harmony and prosperity.' (Norman Davies, *The Isles: A History*, London: Macmillan, 1999, p. 507.) This is done, in part, by presenting the audience with exaggerated stereotypes of English and Continental characters. In Act I Scene II from *The Merchant of Venice* Portia and her lady-in-waiting, Nerissa, are discussing the Englishman, the Scotsman, the Italian, the Frenchman and the two Germans who wish to marry Portia. To win her hand they have to choose between three caskets, one gold, one silver and one lead:

Nerissa: First, there is the Neapolitan prince.
Portia: Ay, there's a colt indeed, for he doth nothing but talk of his horse; and he makes it a great appropriation of his own good parts that he can shoe him himself: I am much afraid my lady his mother played false with a smith.
Nerissa: Then there is the County Palatine.
Portia: He doth nothing but frown: as who should say, An if you will not have me, choose: he hears merry tales and smiles not: I fear he will prove a weeping philosopher when he grows old, being so full of unmannerly sadness in his youth. I had rather be married to a death's head with a bone in his mouth than to either of these. God defend me from these two!
Nerissa: How say you by the French lord, Monsieur Le Bon?

Portia:	God made him, and therefore let him pass for a man. In truth, I know it is a sin to be mocker: but he! why, he hath a horse better than the Neapolitan's; a better bad habit of frowning than the Count Palatine: he is every man and no man; if a throstle sing he falls straight a-capering; he will fence with his own shadow: if I should marry him I should marry twenty husbands. If he would despise me I would forgive him; for if he love me to madness I shall never requite him.
Nerissa:	What say you then to Falconbridge, the young baron of England?
Portia:	You know I say nothing to him; for he understands not me, nor I him: he hath neither Latin, French nor Italian: and you will come into the court and swear that I have a poor pennyworth in the English. He is a proper man's picture; but alas! who can converse with a dumb show? How oddly he is suited! I think, he bought his doublet in Italy, his round hose in France, his bonnet in Germany, and his behaviour everywhere.
Nerissa:	What think you of the Scottish lord, his neighbour?
Portia:	That he hath a neighbourly charity in him; for he borrowed a box of the ear of the Englishman, and swore he would pay him again when he was able: I think the Frenchman became his surety, and sealed under for another.
Nerissa:	How like you the young German, the Duke of Saxony's nephew?
Portia:	Very vilely in the morning when he is sober; and most vilely in the afternoon when he is drunk; when he is best he is a little worse than a man; and when he is worst, he is little better than a beast. An the worst fall that ever fell, I hope I shall make shift to go without him.
Nerissa:	If he should offer to choose the right casket, you should refuse to perform your father's will if you should refuse to accept him.
Portia:	Therefore, for fear of the worst, I pray thee set a deep glass of Rhenish wine on the contrary casket: for if the devil be within and the temptation without, I know he will choose it. I will do anything, Nerissa, ere I will be married to a sponge.

Portia (right) and Nerissa prepare to receive Portia's suitors

Vocabulary

18 recurring (adj.): repeated; happening again and again – **23 environ** (adj.): old form of around – **34 arms** (n. pl.): weapons for fighting wars – **35 naught** (pron.): old form of nothing – **35 to rue** (v.): (literary) to wish you had not done s.th. – **36 to rest** (v.): (archaic) stay, remain – **40 bastard** (adj.): born to parents who are not married – **54 medieval** (adj.): /ˌmediˈiːvəl/ connected with the Middle Ages, the period between about AD 1100 and 1500 – **58 exaggerated** (adj.): if s.th. is exaggerated it is described as better, larger, etc. than it really is – **67 ay** (adv.): a word meaning yes – **67 colt** (n.): young male horse, here: a young man with bad manners – **69 appropriation** (n.): here: addition – **69 parts** (n. pl.): (archaic) abilities – **71 to play false with** (v.): here: to have sex with s.o. who is not your wife or husband – **73 doth** (v.): old form of does – **73 to frown** (v.): to make an angry, unhappy, or confused expression, moving your eyebrows together – **73 as who should say:** (archaic) as if to say – **75 smiles not:** – (archaic) does not smile – **76 weeping** (adj.): (literary) crying – **77 unmannerly** (adj.): (archaic) not having good manners – **85 mocker** (n.): s.o. who laughs at s.o. and tries to make them look stupid by saying unkind things about them – **90 throstle** (n.): (archaic) song thrush, a brown bird with spots on its front – **91 to fence** (v.): to fight with a long thin sword – **94 to despise** (v.): to dislike and have a low opinion of s.o. – **96 to requite** (v.): here: to return feelings of love – **99 baron** (n.): a man who is a member of a low rank of the English nobility – **105 alas** (interj.): (archaic) used to express sadness – **106 to converse** (v.): (fml.) to have a conversation with – **106 dumb show** (n.): here: s.o. who cannot talk – **107 suited** (adj.): here: dressed – **107 doublet** (n.): /ˈdʌblɪ̬t/ a man's tight jacket, worn from about 1400 to the middle 1600s – **108 round hose** (n.): a type of short trousers worn from about 1400 to the middle 1600s – **108 bonnet** (n.): here: cap or hat – **116 surety** (n.): (fml.) s.o. who will pay a debt or s.th. owing if s.o. else fails to do so – **119 vilely** (adv.): here: not at all – **124 to make shift** (v.) (archaic) to find a way of doing s.th. – **125 to offer** (v.) (archaic) to try

– **125 casket** (n.): here: small box – **129 to set** (v.): (archaic) to put – **129 Rhenish** (adj.): coming from the Rhineland – **130 contrary** (adj.): here: wrong – **132 ere** (conj.): (archaic) before – **133 sponge** (n.): a soft natural substance full of small holes which can suck up liquid and is used for cleaning

Explanations

53 Tudor England: England under the Tudor dynasty from the reign of Henry VII in 1485 to the death of Elizabeth I in 1603 – **66 Neapolitan:** coming from the city of Naples in southern Italy – **72 County Palatine:** archaic for a high ranking nobleman, a count – **78 I had rather be:** (archaic) I would rather be – **81 how say you by:** (archaic) what is your opinion of – **89f. he is every man and no man:** he copies everyone but has no personality of his own – **90f. he falls straight a-capering:** (archaic) he immediately starts dancing about – **94 if:** even if – **98 what say you to:** (archaic) what is your opinion of – **104 I have a poor pennyworth in the English:** (archaic) I cannot speak English very well – **105 he is a proper man's picture:** (archaic) he is good-looking – **110 what think you of:** (archaic) what do you think of – **112 a neighbourly charity:** (archaic) a love of his neighbours – **113 a box of the ear:** (archaic) a blow or punch on the side of the head – **116 sealed under for another:** here: promised to do s.th. for s.o. else – **117 how like you?:** (archaic) how do you like? – **123 the worst fall that ever fell:** (archaic) if the worst thing happens – **125 the right casket:** Portia's suitors must choose between three caskets of gold, silver and lead; whoever chooses the one intended by Portia's father wins Portia. – **128 I pray:** (archaic) I ask – **128 thee:** (archaic) you

AWARENESS
1. Describe what do you think of as a "typical" Englishman or Englishwoman, Scotsman or Scotswoman, Frenchman or Frenchwoman, Italian, Spaniard?
2. Write a similar portrait of a "typical" German. What were the sources of the characteristics you used to describe the sterotypes above?

COMPREHENSION
3. Write a brief characterisation of Portia's four suitors in modern English.

OPINION
4. Choose a number of European countries and describe the stereotypes that exist of their inhabitants in Germany. Distinguish between negative and positive stereotypes.

PROJECT
5. Investigate the historical origins of the stereotypes you described in Task 4).

National stereotypes in an English comic

4 George Mikes

How to be an Alien

Even though it was first published in 1946, Hungarian-born George Mikes' book *How to be an Alien* is still a fascinating and highly popular study in intercultural confrontation. By 1977 the picture Mikes had painted of Britain and the British in it was becoming increasingly obsolete and so he wrote a sequel, *How to be Decadent*, not a guide to moral decay, but to life in Britain in the 1970s. This new book now also looks dated, as any visitor to Britain will confirm. The two books are therefore not just two perceptive and very funny descriptions of British life and customs but are testimony to the rapid pace of cultural change within a country. – George Mikes, *How to be an Alien* (London: André Deutsch, 1964), pp. 14 f., pp 26 ff., p. 29.

A WARNING TO BEGINNERS

In England* everything is the other way round. On Sundays on the Continent even the poorest person puts on his best suit, tries to look respectable, and at the same time the life of the country becomes gay and cheerful; in England even the richest peer or motor-manufacturer dresses in some peculiar rags, does not shave, and the country becomes dull and dreary. On the Continent there is one topic which should be avoided – the weather; in England, if you do not repeat the phrase 'Lovely day, isn't it?' at least two hundred times a day, you are considered a bit dull [...] On the Continent people use a fork as though a fork were a shovel; in England they turn it upside down and push everything – including peas – on top of it. [...]

On the Continent stray cats are judged individually on their merit – some are loved, some are only respected; in England they are universally worshipped as in ancient Egypt. On the Continent people have good food; in England people have good table manners. [...]

Continental people are sensitive and touchy; the English take everything with an exquisite sense of humour – they are only offended if you tell them they have no sense of humour. On the Continent the population consists of a small percentage of criminals, a small percentage of honest people and the rest are a vague transition between the two; in England you find a small percentage of criminals and the rest are honest people. On the other hand, people on the Continent either tell you the truth or lie; in England they hardly ever lie, but they would not dream of telling you the truth.

Many continentals think that life is a game; the English think cricket is a game.

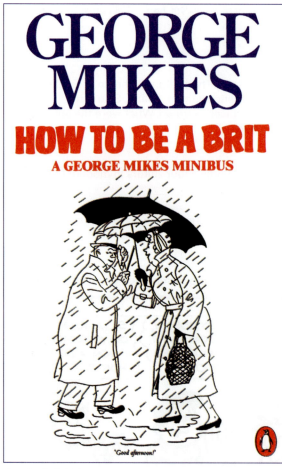

A typically British scene

TEA

The trouble with tea is that originally it was quite a good drink.

So a group of the most eminent British scientists put their heads together, and made complicated biological experiments to find a way of spoiling it.

To the eternal glory of British science their labour bore fruit. They suggested that if you did not drink it clear, or with lemon or rum or sugar, but poured a few drops of cold milk into it, and no sugar at all, the desired object is achieved. Once this refreshing, aromatic, oriental beverage was successfully transformed into colourless and tasteless gargling water, it suddenly became the national drink of Great Britain and Ireland – still retaining, indeed usurping, the high-sounding title of tea. [...]

If you are invited to an English home, at five o'clock in the morning you get a cup of tea. It is either brought in by a heartily smiling hostess or an almost malevolently silent maid. [...]

Then you have tea for breakfast; then you have tea at eleven o'clock in the morning; then after lunch; then you have tea for tea; then after supper; then again at eleven at night.

I have coffee for breakfast; I drink innumerable cups of black coffee during the day; I have the most unorthodox teas even at tea-time. [...]

The other day, for instance – I just mention this as a terrifying example to show you how low some people can sink – I wanted a cup of coffee and a piece of cheese for tea. It was one of those exceptionally hot days and my wife (once a good Englishwoman, now completely and hopelessly led astray by my wicked foreign influence) made some cold coffee and put it in the refrigerator, where it froze and became one solid block. On the other hand, she left the cheese on the kitchen table, where it melted. So I had a piece of coffee and a glass of cheese.

SEX
Continental people have sex life; the English have hot-water bottles.

*When people say England, they sometimes mean Great Britain, sometimes the United Kingdom, sometimes the British Isles – but never England.

Thirty years later ...
George Mikes, *How to be Decadent* (Harmondsworth, Penguin,1981), pp. 12f., p. 23, p.38, p. 65f.

Once upon a time I committed another little book, called *How to be an Alien*. A good friend, to my horror, discovered in 1976 that that book was thirty years old. I have reluctantly to admit that although I was only four years old when I wrote it, this makes me almost middle-aged.

What has changed in thirty years? Who has changed in thirty years? Could I write that book again? If I did try to write it, in what way would it differ from the original *How to be an Alien*?

Both I and Britain have, of course, changed a great deal. First of all, I have become, in a sense, more British than the British while the British have become less British. I have become a little better off than the young refugee was thirty years ago, Britain has become much poorer. I have climbed up the ladder a bit, Britain has climbed down quite a lot. I have become less of a European, Britain – apparently – more European. Britain has lost an Empire and gained me (the net gain, let's face it, is infinitesimal).

How to be an Alien was addressed to fellow aliens, telling them how to make themselves acceptable, how to imitate the English – in other, simple words *How to be an Alien* was telling them how not to be an Alien. [...]

FOOD
'On the Continent people have good food; in England they have good table manners,' I wrote in *How to be an Alien*. Since then, food in England has improved, table manners have deteriorated. In those days food was hardly ever discussed, it was taboo, like sex. Today newspapers and magazines all have their good food guides and many so-called experts send you off to eat uneatable meals. Then it was possible for a much-travelled businessman, even a diplomat, to have no idea what an avocado pear was; today any docker may quarrel with his wife: 'What's that Doris, paella? Paella again? All right, I know I like paella but paella every day – bloody paella and nothing else? What about a decent, honest-to-goodness ratatouille for a change? [...]

SEX
People have asked me many times – with an ironical glint in their eyes – if I still believed (as I wrote in 1946) that 'Continental people have sex-life; the English have hot water bottles.' Or do I agree that things have changed and progressed? Yes, I agree, things have progressed. Not on the Continent, where people still have sex-lives; but they have progressed here because the English now have electric blankets. It is a pity that elecricity so often fails in this country.

[...] Girls are still being taken to bed, to be sure, but they are not courted; they are being made love to but they are not pursued. Women are quite willing to go to bed but they rarely flirt with men. Ladies between the ages of eight and eighty (let's say eighty-five) come back from Italy outraged and complaining bitterly about the crude wolf-whistles. Crude they may be, but they do make middle-aged ladies feel twenty-five years younger, wanted and desired, and these complaints are just disguised boasts. When bishops, retired brigadiers or at least young executives start wolf-whistling in this town of ours, then I may believe that London has become – well, not the sex capital of the world – but a budding sex village.

ON FIDDLING THROUGH
You can be as rude about the English as you wish, they positively like it. In any case you cannot be as rude about them as they are about themselves [...]

It is praising the English that creates problems. Praising is 'patronising', 'slapping on the back', and that they find offensive. Tell them 'you are a great nation' and most of them will laugh because no one has spoken of 'great nations' in Europe since the death of de Gaulle. Others will not laugh but will feel offended: who the hell are you to distribute medals? If you want to be polite, call them a 'once great nation' – or better still: 'a once great nation now in decline'. If you want to flatter them, call them lazy, indolent, inefficient, inept and left behind even by Luxemburg and Andorra. Bernard Shaw made a fortune by calling the English stupid and repeating the charge for six decades, because cleverness is a virtue they particularly despise.

A nice cup of tea …

… or a nice cup of coffee?

Vocabulary

Intro: alien (n.): foreigner, s.o. who is not a legal citizen of the country they are living in – **Intro: sequel** (n.): a book, film, play, that continues the story of an earlier one – **Intro: testimony** (n.): a statement that shows clearly that s.th. is true – **12 peer** (n.): a member of the British nobility or aristocracy – **77 beverage** (n.): a hot or cold drink – **78 gargling** (adj.): being used to clean the inside of your mouth and throat by blowing air through it in the back of your throat – **80 to usurp** (v.): /juːˈzɜːp/ here: to take s.th. you have no right to have – **84 malevolently** (adv.): wanting to harm other people – **88 tea** (n.): here: a small meal of cake or biscuits in the afternoon with a cup of tea; for many people tea is also the name of a large meal eaten early in the evening – **126 better off** (adj.): having more money than you had before – **132 infinitesimal** (adj.): very small – **141 to deteriorate** (v.): to become worse – **148** *paella* (n. sp.): a Spanish dish made with rice, fish, pieces of meat, and vegetables – **150 bloody** (adj.): used to emphasise what you are saying in a rude way – **151 honest-to-goodness** (adj.): simple and good – **151** *ratatouille* (n. fr.): a French dish made with onions, courgettes, tomatoes, aubergines and peppers – **155 glint** (n.): a look in s.o.'s eyes which shows a particular feeling – **164 to court** (v.): to have a romantic relationship with s.o. in the expectation of getting married – **168 to outrage** (v.): to make s.o. feel very angry – **169 wolf-whistle** (n.): a way of whistling that men sometimes use to show that they think a woman is attractive – **172 brigadier** (n.): a high-ranking officer in the British army – **176 budding** (adj.): beginning to develop – **182 patronising** (adj.): s.o. who is patronising talks to you in a way that shows that you are less intelligent or less important than they are – **189 to flatter** (v.): to praise s.o. in order to please them or get s.th. from them – **190 indolent** (adj.): lazy – **190 inept** (adj.): not good at doing s.th. – **192 charge** (n.): statement that s.o. is guilty of a crime or wrongdoing – **194 to despise** (v.): to dislike and have a low opinion of s.o. or s.th.

Explanations

185 de Gaulle: Charles (1890–1970), French general and statesman, head of government 1944–6, President 1959–69. A wartime organiser of the Free French movement outside German-occupied France. – **191 Bernard Shaw:** George Bernard Shaw (1856–1950), Irish dramatist and writer. Notable works are *Man and Superman* (1903), *Pygmalion* (1913) and *St Joan* (1923); he was awarded the Nobel Prize for Literature in 1925.

AWARENESS

1 What warnings about how to behave in Germany would you give to someone from abroad who was going to come and live in your country?

COMPREHENSION

2 What does Mikes consider to be the main differences between life in England and on the Continent?
3 What, according to Mikes, changed in England in the 30 years that passed since he wrote *How to be an Alien*?

ANALYSIS

4 What characteristics of Mikes' texts do you think contributed to making them so hugely popular?
5 Analyse the humour of the text.

OPINION

6 What is your opinion of Mikes' comments on how people behave on the "Continent"?
7 Write an article for a newspaper in which you explain to foreigners how they should behave in Germany.

INTERNET PROJECT

8 It is now another thirty years since George Mikes wrote *How to be Decadent*. Using the websites below as well as newspaper articles find out how England and the English have changed in that time.
www.statistics.gov.uk website of the Office of National Statistics
www.britishembassy.de website of the British Embassy in Germany
www.ipsos-mori.com a market research company which carries out research for advertising and marketing purposes; it includes a social research institute with fascinating information on the attitudes of the British population towards a wide range of issues: Christmas, the Royal Family, politics, Europe, religion, etc.
www.crest.ox.ac.uk an independent academic research organisation (Centre for Research into Elections and Social Trends) which, as well as election behaviour, studies how British social attitudes are changing and how they differ from those in other countries.
The websites of the national newspapers are a useful source of articles on social trends.

5 Sir Owen Seaman

"The Englishman on the French Stage"

This amusing poem deals with a situation that any expatriate can easily identify with: your behaviour is often judged according to the host population's stereotypes of your nation rather than your own character, i.e. anything you do is "typically *****". If you do not act according to those stereotypes, the host population will be terribly disappointed, or you will be considered an untypical eccentric. Seaman takes the situation to its comical extreme: his Englishman constructs a special English identity solely for the purpose of satisfying a French "audience". The obsolete image of an Englishman presented here will nevertheless still strike a chord with many people in Britain and Europe, such is the power of the stereotype created in literature and popular culture at the end of the 19th century. – *The Oxford Book of Travel Verse*, ed. by Kevin Crossley-Holland (Oxford: Oxford University Press, 1986), p. 53f.

1 When I'm in France, for Frenchmen's sake
   It is my rule to wear
What in their innocence they take
   To be a British air.

5 I like to feel, when our Allies
   My dress and manners scan,
That they can readily surmise,
   'There goes an Englishman.'

But, since they never cross the wave
10   To get the facts correct –
How Englishmen this side behave,
   What suiting we affect –

I have to imitate the type
   Dear to the Paris stage,
15 Hallowed by humorous mimes and ripe
   With immemorial age.

In chequered tweeds I go all day,
   Loud stockings on my legs;
And for my early déjeuner
   I order ham and eggs.   20

On cheeks habitually nude
   Red whiskers I emplace,
And make my frontal teeth protrude
   Some way outside my face.

A kodak and a bright-red guide   25
   In either arm I hug,
As down the boulevard's length I stride,
   Emitting blasts of plug.

My hobnails on the pavement ring;
   My brogues are caked with loam;   30
I read The Daily Tale – a thing
   I rarely do at home.

Strange slang and unfamiliar oaths
  My conversation spice;
35 I ask for what my body loathes –
  A morning tub of ice.

When gardiens lift their voices high
  Some trespass to condemn,
To their gesticulations I
40 Oppose a perfect phlegm.

Enfin (in fine), when I'm in France
  I try my best to do
In every circumstance
  What they expect me to.

45 It keeps the Entente fresh and hot
  To recognize in me
Its unimpaired ideal of what
  An Englishman should be.

Sir Owen Seaman (1861–1936) was a British writer,
50 journalist and poet. He joined the staff of the humorous magazine *Punch* in 1897 and edited the magazine from 1906 to 1932.

Wilhelm Busch's idea of a typical Englishman (1882)

Vocabulary

3 innocence (n.): here: not having experience of life or knowledge of the world – **4 air** (n.): appearance, the way s.o. looks to other people – **7 to surmise** (v.) /səˈmaɪz/: (fml.) to guess that s.th. is true – **9 wave** (n.): here: water between England and France – **12 suiting** (n.): material used for making suits – **12 to affect** (v.): here: to use, wear s.th. in order to make a particular impression on s.o. – **14 stage** (n.): here: theatre – **15 hallowed** (adj.): (fml.) here: made known and respected by being repeated many times – **15 mime** (n.): here: play in a theatre – **15 ripe** (adj.): here: accepted – **18 loud** (adj.): here: with many bright colours – **19 déjeuner** (fr. n.): here: breakfast – **21 habitually** (adv.): usually – **21 nude** (adj.): here: without any hair on – **22 to emplace** (v.): (fml.) here: to put, let grow – **23 to protrude** (v.): to stick out – **28 to emit** (v.): to send out – **28 plug** (n.): here: piece of tobacco used for chewing – **29 hobnail** (n.): here: a large heavy boot with nails at the bottom – **30 brogue** (n.): a thick strong leather shoe with a pattern in the leather – **30 caked** (adj.): covered – **30 loam** (n.): here: mud – **33 oath** (n.): here: a rude word or phrase that expresses anger, surprise, or shock – **34 to spice** (v.): to add interest or excitement to s.th. – **35 to loathe** (v.): to hate s.th. or s.o. very much – **38 trespass** (n.): here:: s.th. that you have done that is wrong – **40 phlegm** (n.) /flem/: here: being calm in worrying, frightening or exciting situations – **47 unimpaired** (adj.): not damaged

Explanations

5 Allies (n.): here: the French; see Entente – **11 this side**: here: on the French side of the English Channnel – **25 kodak** (fr. n.): in French the trade name Kodak is used for a small simple box camera – **25 bright-red guide**: a reference to the guide books for hotels and restaurants produced by the Michelin Tyre Company – **31 The Daily Tale**: a fictional English newspaper – **37 gardiens** (fr. n.): gardiens de la paix; French police officer – **41 enfin** (fr. adv.): at last; translated incorrectly as a joke by the writer – **45 Entente** (n.): a friendly understanding; the expression Entente Cordiale refers to the informal understanding and series of agreements between Britain and France reached in 1904 which formed the basis for Britain's entry into the First World War on the side of France and Russia against Germany and the Austro-Hungarian Empire. The hundredth anniversary of the Entente Cordiale in 2004 was marked by a number of official and unofficial events. The anniversary commemorative website is at http://www.entente-cordiale.org/.

Awareness
1. What do you think of as a "typical" Englishman?

Comprehension
2. Why don't the French really know what the English are like?
3. Where do the French get their English stereotypes from?
4. What are, for the French, the characteristics of a "typical" Englishman?
5. What is the motive behind the Englishman's attempt to fit in with the French strereotype of the English?

Analysis
6. How does the Englishman in the poem change his behaviour to fit in with French ideas of what an Englishman should be?
7. Analyse the humour of the poem.

Opinion
8. Imagine you were living in a foreign country. What pressures on you to modify your behaviour would there be and how far and in what way would you change you behaviour?

Project
9. Investigate the way German newspapers and magazines present the English, Welsh and Scots and so contribute to the German image of a "typical" British person.

Stephen Clarke

An Englishman in Paris*

Paul West has, like many thousands of British people, moved to Europe to set up his own business, in his case an English tea shop. He is soon confronted with French bureaucracy and its many demands on employers and business people. One of them is the requirement that all business and advertising material should be written in French. – Stephen Clarke, *Merde Actually* (London: Bantam Press, 2005), pp. 276–281.

1   It was late, just before closing time, and I was resting my feet, reading the newspaper over a cup of Orange Pekoe. I didn't really pay any attention to the guy at first, except to do a double-take at his impeccable
5   colour coordination. Sand-brown fleece, beige-and-green shirt, khaki chinos, light brown suede shoes. Even his hair matched, a kind of chestnut-and-grey flecked combination. Here, I felt, was a guy whose sock drawer was graded in a strict spectrum pattern.
10   I returned to reading the football pages. [...]
But my attention wandered back to the sock-drawer man again when I realized that he was arguing loudly with Benoît, who wasn't an arguing-loudly kind of guy.
15   'You must translate everything,' the sock-drawer guy was saying. 'Cup of tea, for example.'
'But every French person knows what a cup of tea is.'

'How do you know this? Perhaps I do not know this?'   20
'Don't you know what a cup of tea is?'
'No.'
'Yes you do, you ordered one when you came in.'
'Perhaps I was just curious to know what this unknown thing was on the menu.'   25
I realized I had to intervene. Benoît was clearly up against a mind more fiendish than he could possibly imagine. A French bureaucratic mind.
I introduced myself and asked him what the problem was.   30
The guy didn't introduce himself. He simply snapped back a question, in French of course. 'What is a moog?'
'Moog?'
'Oui, moog of tea.'   35
'Ah, mug,' I corrected him.

'Oui, mag.'
'Mug.'
'Mog.'
'Mug.'
'Maaahg.'

'Oui, c'est ça,' I congratulated him. 'Un maaahhg est un grand coop.'

'Coop?'

'Cup.'

He snorted triumphantly. 'You see, even you do not know what a cup is. That is why you must translate it as tasse de thé. You must translate everything on your menu.'

He introduced himself as an inspector from the Ministère de la Francophonie, the government department that tries to protect the French language from attack by such invaders as 'le marketing', 'le Walkman' and, it seemed, 'le cup of tea'.

He flashed his ID card at a wide-eyed Benoît and me and informed us that it was illegal to have a menu that did not give French translations for every foreign ingredient or dish.

'What, even sandwich?' I asked. I pronounced it à la française; 'son-dweetch', though the French spell the word as in English.

'No, of course not.'

'OK, so if it is an English word that is used in French, or known by the French, I don't have to translate it.'

'English? But sandwich is French.' His cheeks flushed for a moment, but realized they were disrupting his colour scheme and quickly returned to their normal shade of grey-green.

'What? Sandwich is English.'

'Ho!' This was by no means a laugh. It was a cry of indignation. He appealed for support to Benoît, but by this time the poor lad was gaping at us mutely, stroking the tea urn for moral support. 'It is like les frites,' – French fries – the inspector went on. 'The whole world knows they are French, except the English who say they invented them. As do the Belgians, but who cares about them? We French have been eating sandwiches for much longer than you. The traditional baguette is the perfect bread for a sandwich.'

Apart from his wild rewriting of culinary history, he'd left himself open to attack here, and I darted in.

'No it's not. It's the worst bread in the world for a sandwich. You can't get it in your mouth.' I mimed the impossible task of closing your teeth on a baguette sandwich without first crushing it flat. 'And when you squeeze it, all the ingredients fall out the other end of the sandwich on to your trousers.'

His eyes narrowed at me. 'I thought we were having a linguistic conversation, Monsieur, not criticizing French table manners.' When a Frenchman uses 'Monsieur' at you in the middle of an argument, you know you've offended him badly.

'I wasn't criticizing French table manners,' I assured him. 'But sandwich really is an English word.'

'Nonsense. What is its meaning? Something to do with sand, no doubt?'

'It's the name of the man who invented it.'

'Ah oui. Monsieur Sandwich, a cousin of Monsieur Fish and Chips?' He bowed as if acknowledging polite applause at his rapier wit. Even Benoît accorded him a nod of appreciation.

I could see that I was rapidly sinking into the quicksand of an intellectual discussion that was only going to drag me under. This guy was a professional quibbler, after all. His clothes and his ID badge proved it.

And as everyone knows, once you're in quicksand, the last thing you should do is flail about and hope you can fight your way out.

Trouble is, some of us are just born flailers.

'Well, it's an English word so I'm going to translate it on my menu,' I told him.

'You will not translate it. It is French.'

'It is an English word and I demand the right to translate it.'

'I forbid you to translate it.' By this time we were practically nose to nose.

'I will translate it as "traditional English food with two slices of bread and, er, something between".' My French let me down at the end but the blow struck home.

'That would be a gross misrepresentation. The law forbids incorrect translations.'

'Oh yes? Well we shall see what Bruxelles says about that. Or Brussel as the Flemish residents call it. Bruxelles is just a bad translation, n'est-ce pas?'

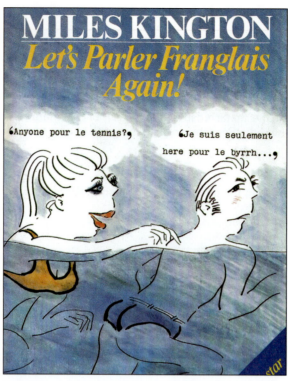

MILES KINGTON
Let's Parler Franglais Again!

Franglais – a humorous mixture of French and English and a topic of several funny books, but no help in communicating with French officials

The inspector took up the gauntlet and threw it back in my face. 'I will return, and if there is one mistake in the French translations on your menu, you will be obliged to reprint all of them, or face a heavy fine.'

No one throws gauntlets in my face and gets away with it, even if my face is the only part of me still sticking up out of the quicksand. 'Oh yes?' I replied. 'We will take the train together to Brussel to discuss the case.'

As the glass door clanged shut behind him, I'm sure both of us were feeling that peculiarly French sense of satisfaction at having created mutual outrage. Nothing at all had been resolved, but we'd had a damn good row and each of us had emerged feeling sure we were in the right. I was as exhilarated as a poodle strutting away after a damn good yapping match.

Vocabulary

4 to do a double-take (v.): to look at s.o. or s.th. again because you are very surprised by what you saw or heard – **4 impeccable** (adj.): without any faults – **6 chinos** (n. pl.) /'tʃiːnəʊz/: loose trousers made from strong woven cotton – **6 suede** (adj.) /sweɪd/: made of soft leather with a slightly rough surface – **26f. to be up against** (v.): to have to deal with – **27 fiendish** (adj.) /'fiːndɪʃ/: here: very clever in an unpleasant way – **31f. to snap back** (v.): here: answer quickly in an angry way – **37 to snort** (v.): to breathe air in a noisy way out through your nose, esp. to show you are annoyed or amused – **65 to flush** (v.): to become red in the face – **65 to disrupt** (v.): to prevent s.th. from continuing in its usual way – **71 to gape** (v.): to look at s.th. or s.o. for a long time with your mouth open because you are surprised or shocked – **71 mutely** (adv.): silently – **72 urn** (n.): a metal container that holds a large amount of tea or coffee – **80 to dart** (v.): to move suddenly and quickly – **112 to acknowledge** (v.): to show s.o. that you have noticed them – **113 rapier** (adj.): here: sharp – **113 to accord** (v.): here: (fml.): to give – **117 to drag** (v.): here: to make s.o. feel unhappy – **118 quibbler** (n.): s.o. who argues about small unimportant details – **120 quicksand** (n.): wet sand that is dangerous because you sink down into it if you try to walk on it – **121 to flail about** (v.): to wave your arms in an uncontrolled way – **133 to let s.o. down** (v.): to make s.o. be less successful – **133 to strike home** (v.): to have the effect on s.o. you intended – **134 gross** (adj.): here: very wrong and unacceptable – **134 misrepresentation** (n.): a wrong description of a situation – **139 to take up the gauntlet** (v.): to accept the invitation to fight – **150 mutual** (adj.): mutual feelings are feelings that two or more people have for each other – **150 outrage** (n.): a feeling of great anger – **153 exhilarated** (adj.): feeling extemely happy – **153 to strut** (v.): to walk proudly with your head high and chest pushed forward – **154 yapping** (adj.): here: noisy like a dog barking

Explanations

13 Benoît: French waiter at Paul West's tea shop – **46f. Ministère de la Francophonie:** the – fictional – French ministry responsible for seeing that French is used in France (see Info Box below) – **54 ID card:** document that shows your name and date of birth, usually with a photograph – **58 sandwich:** named after the 4th Earl of Sandwich, an English nobleman said to have eaten food within two slices of bread so as not to leave the gambling table

"Ministère de la Francophonie"

In fact it is the Ministère de la Culture et de la Communication which is responsible for making laws to ensure that French is used in France and it was the law of 4 August 1994 which lays down policy for the use of French. The criteria for the use of so-called foreign words and their French equivalents – CRITER – can be found under: www.culture.gouv.fr/culturedglf/terminlogie/base-donnee.html. If the words sandwich and weekend are typed in, no French equivalent is given, whereas if the terms computer and monitor are typed in, the French equivalents *ordinateur* and *moniteur* are given. All French equivalents listed are, according to a decree of 3 July 1996, compulsory for use in state organisations.

AWARENESS
1 Discuss the type of business that you might be able to set up in another European country. What kinds of products or services could you offer?

COMPREHENSION
2 Why has the French official come to Paul West's café?
3 What is it about the French official's appearance that Paul West finds particularly striking?
4 Why does the French official think that "sandwich" (l. 58) is a French word?

ANALYSIS
5 Analyse the interaction between Paul West and the French official. Look at the following points: a) how they address each other; b) who asks questions and how the questions are expressed; c) how the questions are answered; d) how the two men express their French and English identities and respond to the identity of the other; e) show how the confrontation develops into a row.
6 What, seen from Paul West's point of view, is particularly French about the French official?
7 What, by implication, is particularly English about Paul West?
8 What role does the incorrect pronunciation of English words play in the text?

OPINION
9 Write a dialogue between Paul West and the French official in which the two men do not have a row and part on friendly terms.
10 Write a polemical essay in which you either a) defend the right of speakers of French and German to use English words and phrases whenever they wish or b) make a case for protecting French and German from the use of English words and phrases. Use your essays as the basis for a class discussion on the use of English words and phrases in French and German.

INTERNET PROJECT
11 Look up the French websites concerned with the protection of French and write a short description of French government language policies.

'Ici on parle Anglais' … 'Ici on se rit de votre français.' ('We speak English here' … 'We laugh at your French here'.)

7 Robert Southey
"After Blenheim"

Rather than celebrate a great English victory over the French, the Battle of Blenheim, Robert Southey chose to write what is considered to be the first anti-war poem. The battle, fought on 13 August 1704 and known in Germany as the Battle of Hochstädt, was a turning point in the War of the Spanish Succession. The combatants were troops from Austria, England and the United Provinces, commanded by the Duke of Marlborough and Prince Eugene of Savoy, who fought against troops from France and Bavaria under Count Camille de Tallard and Maximilian II Emanuel, the Elector of Bavaria. The name Blenheim is the anglicised version of Blindheim, in Bavaria. – From: *The Faber Book of Political Verse* ed. by Tom Paulin (London: Faber and Faber, 1986), pp. 224–6.

1

1 It was on a summer evening,
    Old Kaspar's work was done,
And he before his cottage door
    Was sitting in the sun,
5 And by him sported on the green
His little grandchild Wilhelmine.

2

She saw her brother Peterkin
    Roll something large and round,
Which he beside the rivulet
10   In playing there had found;
He came to ask what he had found,
That was so large, and smooth, and round.

3

Old Kaspar took it from the boy,
    Who stood expectant by;
15 And then the old man shook his head
    And with a natural sigh,
'Tis some poor fellow's skull', said he,
'Who fell in the great victory.

4

'I find them in the garden,
20   For there's many here about;
And often when I go to plough,
    The ploughshare turns them out!
For many thousand men', said he,
'Were slain in that great victory.'

5

25 'Now tell us what 't was all about,'
    Young Peterkin, he cries;
And little Wilhelmine looks up
    With wonder-waiting eyes;
'Now tell us all about the war,
30 And what they fought each other for.'

John Churchill, Duke of Marlborough

6

'It was the English', Kaspar cried,
    Who put the French to rout;
But what they fought each other for,
    I could not well make out;
But everybody said', quoth he,
'That 't was a famous victory.

7

'My father lived at Blenheim then,
    Yon little stream hard by;
They burnt his dwelling to the ground,
    And he was forced to fly;
So with his wife and child he fled,
Nor had he where to rest his head.

8

'With fire and sword the country round
    Was wasted far and wide,
And many a childling mother then,
    And new-born baby died;
But things like that, you know, must be
At every famous victory.

9

'They say it was a shocking sight
    After the field was won;
For many thousand bodies here
    Lay rotting in the sun;
But things like that, you know, must be
After a famous victory.

10

'Great praise the Duke of Marlbro' won,
    And our good Prince Eugene.'
'Why 't was a very wicked thing!'
    Said little Wilhelmine.
'Nay .. nay .. my little girl', quoth he,
'It was a famous victory.

11

'And everybody praised the Duke
    Who this great fight did win.'
'But what good came of it at last?'
    Quoth little Peterkin.
'Why I cannot tell,' said he,
But 't was a famous victory.'

Westbury, 1798

Robert Southey (1774–1843) was born in Bristol on August 12, 1774, the son of a linen draper. He was sent to Westminster School in London where he began to write. He was expelled from there after writing an article for the school magazine criticising the system of corporal punishment used at the school. He then studied at Balliol College, Oxford, where he said that he learned two things: how to row and how to swim. After leaving Oxford without a degree he met the poet Samuel Taylor Coleridge who shared his sympathy for the French Revolution. Together they wrote the topical drama *The Fall of Robespierre* (1794). His ardent support of the French Revolution was expressed in his poem *Joan of Arc* (1796). From 1797 onwards he earned his living as a writer and produced a stream of works in a wide range of genres: poetry (the best-known being *The Inchcape Rock* and *After Blenheim*), stories (including most notably the children's story *The Three Bears*), criticism, history, biography (including a life of Nelson, still regarded as a classic), journalism, translations and editions of earlier writers. In 1813 he was appointed poet laureate (the poet chosen by the monarch and who writes poems on important national occasions).

Vocabulary

5 to sport (v.): here: to play – **5 green** (n.): a level area of grass – **9 rivulet** (n.): here: a small river – **17 skull** (n.): the bones of a person's head – **21 to plough** (v.) /plaʊ/: to turn over the earth with the tool called a plough so that seeds can be planted – **22 ploughshare**: the metal blade of a plough – **24 slain** (p.p. of to slay): killed – **28 wonder-waiting** (adj.): waiting full of admiration and surprise – **32 to put to rout** (v.): to defeat s.o. completely in a battle – **35 to quoth** (v.): (archaic) to say – **38 yon** (det.): (archaic) over there – **38 hard by** (prep.): (archaic) very near – **39 dwelling** (n.): (fml.) a house where people live – **40 to fly** (v.): (fml.) to leave somewhere in order to escape; to flee – **41 fled** (past tense of to flee): escaped – **44 to waste** (v.): (fml.) to destroy or damage s.th. esp. in war – **45 childling** (adj.): (archaic): with an unborn baby growing inside her body

Explanations

Intro: The War of the Spanish Succession (1701–14): this war between the Grand Alliance of England, Holland, and the Holy Roman Empire on the one hand and France, Spain, and Bavaria on the other, broke out after the death of Charles II, the last Spanish Habsburg king. The cause of the war was the conflict between the powers concerned over who should get the Spanish dominions. – **7 Peterkin**: the boy's name is Peter; the ending -kin is added to show he is small or young – **17 tis**: (archaic) it is – **25 't**: (archaic) it – **55 Duke of Marlbro'**: abbrev. for Duke of Marlborough, John Churchill (1650–1722) – **56 Prince Eugene**: Prince Eugene of Savoy (1663–1736); although he was French, Prince Eugene entered the service of Holy Roman Emperor, Leopold I. After fighting the Ottoman Turks, he became the principal imperial commander in the War of the Spanish Succession. After defeating the French forces in northern Italy he joined the Duke of Marlborough in Bavaria where they won the victory of Blenheim. – **59 nay**: (archaic) no

AWARENESS

1 Name some great battles in German history and account for their significance.
2 What do you know about the great battles in British history?

ANALYSIS

3 Contrast the view of the battle held by the old man Kaspar and by the children Peterkin and Wilhelmine.
4 What elements of the poem might lead the reader to believe that it was critical of war?
5 What is the effect on the reader of the repetition of the phrase "famous victory"?
6 What is the function of the direct speech in this poem?

OPINION

7 Discuss how far this poem has affected your attitude towards warfare.

PROJECT

8 Compare Robert Southey's poem with two other famous anti-war texts: *Dulce et decorum est* by Wilfried Owen (1918) and Bob Dylan's song *With God on our Side* (1963).

The Battle of Blenheim

Blenheim Palace, Oxfordshire

The Battle of Blenheim was a decisive victory for the Anglo-Dutch-Austrian alliance and the first major English victory in Europe since the Battle of Agincourt in 1415. It was considered one of the pivotal victories in European history since it prevented French domination of Europe under Louis XIV and contributed to the formation of the concept of "Balance of Power". This concept, meaning the prevention of the dominance of Europe by any one power, was first invoked in the Treaty of Utrecht, which concluded the War of Spanish Succession.

The commander of the English forces, John Churchill, the first Duke of Marlborough, was granted the Royal Manor of Woodstock for his part in the victory. The house that he built on the site at Woodstock was named Blenheim Palace after the battle. John Churchill's most famous descendent was Sir Winston Churchill (see Text 12), who was born at Blenheim Palace in 1874.

Background Reading

Battles in European History

Great battles are a defining feature of national and of European identity. They create myths of national achievement and heroism and images of the threatening and aggressive other. The best-known date in Anglo-British history is that of the Battle of Hastings in 1066, when frenchified Norsemen from Normandy destroyed Anglo-Saxon England, an event remembered and regretted until at least the 18th century by those who referred to the 'Norman yoke'. Wars with France, Spain, the Netherlands, and Germany helped define English and later British identity. Wars are no less important for national perceptions of identity in continental Europe. Students could investigate the effects of the Napoleonic Wars on German identity for example. Other interesting lines of enquiry would be to look at the role of battles with non-Europeans in forming European identity: between Greeks and Persians at Thermopylae 480 BC and Salamis 480 BC, between Romans and Carthage in the Punic Wars 264–241, 218–201, 149–146 BC, the defeat of the Emirate of Cordoba's Arab army at the Battle of Tours in 732 AD, the defeat of the Turks at Vienna by John Sobieski, King of Poland, in 1683 – both saving "Europe" from domination by Islam. Yet another interesting task would be to look at the celebration of defeats, most notably that of Dunkirk, May 26 to June 4, 1940 in the Second World War, and the never-ending appeals thereafter in Britain to "the Dunkirk spirit". In Europe the most famous defeat to be celebrated is that of the Battle on the Amselfeld (*Kosovo Polje* – field of the blackbirds) in the Serbian province of Kosovo in 1389, when a Turkish army decisively defeated the Serbs. The battlefield took a central place in Serbian myths of national renewal and this was one reason for Serbia's refusal to consider giving Kosovo, now mainly inhabited by Albanians, any form of national autonomy.

8 Len Deighton

SS-GB

In his excursion into alternative history (see also the Info Box on p. 47), *SS-GB*, Len Deighton describes Britain in 1941, one year after its conquest by German forces. The hero, Douglas Archer, is a high-ranking detective investigating the murder of an atomic scientist. He is caught between the conflicting forces of the British resistance, the German army, the SS, and German counter-intelligence. Like any public servant in an occupied country he finds it a difficult line to walk between collaboration and resistance. He sometimes finds that it is not enough to say that 'The British public have a right to be protected against murder, robbery and violence. Do I have to tell the victims of such crimes that I don't like working under the Germans?'

In the course of his investigations Archer attends a party at the luxurious London home of Sydney Garin, an art dealer who buys and sells paintings and art treasures from and to the occupying Germans. – Len Deighton, *SS-GB* (London: Jonathan Cape, 1978), pp. 102 ff.

While the Tatler and Queen and other high-society gravure magazines were showing how Britain's nobility and country gentry were celebrating their weddings and twenty-first birthdays with toasted cheese snacks and home-made beer, a new class of men had emerged from the wreckage of defeat. Shetland, the hard-eyed aristocrat, and Sydney Garin, one-time Armenian, typified the emergent super-rich. And so did their guest-list.

'Good evening, Douglas,' said Garin as he came into the main hall.

'Good evening, Mr Garin. Good evening, Mrs Garin.'

Garin's wife – a mousy little woman with a bodice full of diamonds and pearls, and tight wavy hair – smiled as if pleased to be noticed. Their son was there too smiling dutifully at each new arrival.

It was to be expected that the Germans would be here; Generals and Admirals and men from the tiny civil administration which – under the command of the military Commander-in-Chief – controlled occupied Britain. And there were Englishmen: Members of Parliament and members of the puppet government who had learned to play their role in the new Nazi super-state that covered most of Europe. The Prime Minister sent his regrets; he was addressing a gathering of German schoolteachers.

Here too were the men of Whitehall; top-ranking bureaucrats whose departments continued to run as smoothly under the German flag as they had under conservative and socialist governments. There were nobility too, placed in the guest list with that seemingly artless skill that a gardener uses with a few blooms that flower in the heart of winter; nobility from Poland, France and Italy as well as the home-grown variety. And always there were businessmen; individuals who could get you a thousand pairs of rubber boots, or a hundred kilometres of electrified fencing; three crosses and nine long nails.

It was like half-awakening from some terrible nightmare, thought Douglas. The long dresses of fine silks and hand embroidery, the carefully tailored evening suits of the men, and the impeccable clothes of the waiters, came as a shock after the cruel and cynical mood of defeat that prevailed beyond those wrought-iron gates and well-kept gravel drive, and the neat lawn that was shiny and pink in the last evening light.

And the voices were different too; quick-witted responses and relaxed movements in these large, warm and comfortable rooms were quite unlike the hushed voices and furtive movements that had become a standard part of British life. But more than anything else Douglas was surprised by the light; there was so much of it and every room was the same. Rich golden light picked out the superb mouldings, the marble mantlepieces and Adam furniture, glittered in the cut-glass chandeliers, and shone through the bubbles in the endless champagne.

It was a magificent house, comparable with Portman House round the corner, containing enough beautiful things to be a museum. And like a museum it was crowded with such objects, so that they were too close together, as if in some monstrous competition of the absolute.

Victory Parade, London, April 20, 1941.
The Führer takes the salute in Whitehall on his 52nd birthday as SS Divisions march past – a fictional scene of alternative history.

At the far end of the ballroom, through two smaller reception rooms, and beyond the folding doors with sixteenth-century flower paintings on the panels, there were spotlights. There, mounted on a specially constructed platform – discreetly clothed in red velvet – was a small fifteenth-century Flemish diptych that Sydney Garin had purchased in Geneva. For this one evening only it was on display for the private pleasure of Garin's invited guests. Tomorrow it was to be crated for delivery to Reichsmarschall Göring's art gallery at Karinhall. In exchange, Garin and Shetland had accepted eight 'decadent' surrealist paintings that Göring had confiscated from non-Aryan owners.

Around the room there were little groups of middle-ranking German officers, self-conscious in their uniforms and awkward in their lack of English language. Here and there some self-appointed spokesman fronted each group, behaving like some travel courier guarding a bunch of elderly tourists. There were high-ranking officers, elderly self-assured men with closely cut grey hair and sometimes monocles, wearing the gold insignia of Admirals on their white mess jackets, or the wide red trouser stripe that denotes the General. Some were accompanied by personal interpreters in the special Sonderführer uniform.

There were girls there too. Plump girls with too much expensive make-up, and dresses that were cut tight across the bottom and deeply at the neckline. Elsewhere in London at this time such girls might have gone unremarked but in this temperate assembly they were conspicuous in a way that perhaps they intended to be. Already such girls had learned how to sandwich together a few German phrases – pronunciation perfect – and when their knowledge of German ran dry, a smile or a laugh would easily do. There were lots of smiles and laughter, and the couples who could not converse together danced instead.

Gathered in a defensive circle, under a magnificent Cranach Crucifixion, Douglas recognised a representative collection of London's new socialites. Upon them fortune had smiled since the night when a German news agency message reported Churchill's request for a cease-fire.

This cartoon appeared soon after BMW abandoned its takeover of the British motor manufacturer Rover in 2000 and it became clear the Rover would not survive

Vocabulary

Intro: counter-intelligence (n.): action a country takes to stop another country discovering its secrets – **Intro: public servant** (n.): s.o. who works for the government – **1f. gravure** (n.): method of printing in which an image from a photographic negative is transferred to a metal plate – **3 gentry** (n.): people who belong to a high social class, esp. those who own land – **5 to emerge** (v.): to appear from somewhere: – **7 one-time** (adj.): former – **8 emergent** (adj.): in the early stages of existence – **12 bodice** (n.): the part of a woman's dress above her waist – **21 puppet** (n.): here: controlled by a more powerful country – **24 to send your regrets** (n.): to say you are unable to go to a meeting – **31 artless** (adj.): (fml.) made or done without any effort – **40 embroidery** (n.): cloth with patterns sewn onto it – **41 impeccable** (adj.): without any faults or marks – **43 to prevail** (v.): (fml.) if s.th. prevails it exists among a group of people at a certain time – **43 wrought-iron** (adj.): long thin pieces of iron formed into shapes to make gates, fences, etc. – **44 gravel** (adj.): small stones used to make paths, roads, etc. – **48 hushed** (adj.): quiet – **49 furtive** (adj.): behaving as if you want to keep s.th. secret – **53 moulding** (n.): a thin decorative line of plaster or wood around the edge of a wall – **63 reception room** (n.): a room where people sit or stand with guests – **69 clothed** (adj.): covered – **69 velvet** (n.): a type of expensive cloth with a soft surface on one side – **70 diptych** (n.): a picture made in two parts that can be closed like a book – **95 mess jacket** (n.): a jacket worn by army, navy or air force officers when they are not on duty – **105 temperate** (adj.): here: calm – **106 conspicuous** (adj.): very easy to notice – **107f. to sandwich together** (v.): here: to manage to say s.th. that other people can understand – **110 to do** (v.): to be enough, acceptable – **115 socialite** (n.): s.o. who is well-known for going to many fashionable parties

Explanations

1 Tatler: originally founded in 1709 as The Tatler, it claims to be the world's oldest magazine. – **1 Queen:** a fashion and society magazine similar to Tatler. – **53f. Adam furniture:** furniture made in the neoclassical style initiated by the Scottish architect, interior designer and furniture designer Robert Adam (1728–92) – **56f. Portman House:** a large house in Portman Street near Oxford Street in the West End of London, now demolished – **72 Geneva:** city in southwest Switzerland – **76 Reichsmarschall Göring:** Hermann Göring (in English also Goering) (1893–1946) Nazi leader and politician, deputy to Adolf Hitler, head of the German air force before and during World War II; the title Reichsmarschall was created especially for him. – **77 Karinhall:** vast Prussian estate and residence belonging to Göring, named after his first wife, Carin von Kantzow – **81 non-Aryan:** according to Nazi race ideology not belonging to the so-called Germanic races – **99 *Sonderführer:*** a special rank in the German army created in 1937 for soldiers who had specialist skills such as translators, interpreters, doctors, but who didn't have the military training for a regular military rank; they were known by normal soldiers as "*Schmalspuroffiziere*". – **114 Cranach Crucifixion:** a painting of the crucifixion of Jesus Christ (1502) by the German painter Lucas Cranach the Elder (1472–1553); the painting can be seen at the Kunsthistorisches Museum in Vienna. – **117 Churchill:** Sir Winston (Leonard Spencer) (1874–1965, British Conservative political leader; prime minister 1940–5 and 1951–5; in the novel *SS-GB* Churchill is taken to Berlin and executed.

Awareness

1. What alternative history novels or stories do you know? What is the motivation behind writing alternative history?

Comprehension

2. What is the implication of the description of the German civil administration of Britain as "tiny" (l. 17)?
3. What is the significance of the phrase "three crosses and nine long nails" (ll. 36f.)?

Analysis

4. Who, to judge by the people at Sydney Garin's party, were the people who had profited from Britain's defeat by the Germans?
5. How does Len Deighton create the special atmosphere at Sydney Garin's party?
6. What indications are there in the text of another, more unpleasant world outside Sydney Garin's luxurious house?

Opinion

7. Many academic historians reject the whole idea of writing alternative history novels as mere fantasising about what never happened. Write an essay in which you either attack the concept of alternative history or defend it.

Project

8. Investigate how feasible a German invasion of Britain would have been in 1940 and why it never took place.

Britain in Europe

9 Bert Trautmann – the German who became an Englishman*

Bert Trautmann was the most famous and popular goalkeeper in England from 1949 to 1969. In this newspaper article he tells how he was taken prisoner by the British in the Second World War, stayed in England, became one of its most popular sportsmen, and came to love the country and its people. – *The Sunday Times,* 7 November 2004, p. 5.5.

Come on England ... the chant of the German goalie

I still shout for England when they're playing. Even though it is years since I was Manchester City's goalie. I was born a German but Britain is the country that made me what I am today. That is why receiving my OBE for services to Anglo-German understanding from the Queen last week meant so much to me.

When I first arrived in England, I used to have to apologise for my past. I hope I don't have to any more; it all started so innocently.

In 1928, at the age of five and living in Bremen, I joined the Falcons, rather like the Boy Scouts, then when Hitler took power in 1933 I joined the Jungvolk, the junior Hitler Youth. We didn't understand the politics of it. We just wanted to play sports and go camping.

I knew very little about what it meant to fight and to kill but at 17 I joined the Luftwaffe. I wanted to be a pilot but I was colour blind, so I became a paratrooper and was drafted to Poland. Then in June 1941 we went into Russia. There was no elation, no triumphalism. I fought in Russia for three terrible years. We lost a million men simply from the cold. I grew up fast. I was captured briefly by the Russians but escaped. I was one of only 90 survivors out of my original 1,000 comrades.

I was made a sergeant and my regiment regrouped near Paris to counter the D-Day landings. We fought through France, Holland, in Arnhem and the Ardennes, then back through Germany, where in 1945 I was again captured, this time by the Americans. Two GIs were ordered to take me to a tree in the middle of a field. I was sure they were going to shoot us but then, and I'll never know why, they just let me go.

I fled and a few days later I scaled a fence – and dropped at the feet of two Tommies. "Hello Fritz," they said. "Fancy a cup of tea?" That was my first encounter

Bert Trautmann was awarded the Footballer of the Year Trophy in 1956

with the British. I had been told they were a horrible race. But I was grateful for the tea and decided not to escape any more.

I was sent to a PoW camp at Ashton-in-Makerfield, in Lancashire, where I was put in a special section for Nazis, so I was among the last to be released. I was there for three years. This was when what I call my "education" started. I learnt what it is to be British. I became a totally different person, more knowledgeable, more tolerant, more understanding.

I played football in the camp, first against other prisoners and then against local English amateur teams. We got to know the Lancashire people quite well and I learnt to speak English. I stopped calling myself Bernhard and became Bert.

After my release in 1948 there was nothing at home for me. My mother and father were still alive but our house had gone in the allied raids on Bremen.

So, to save up for a coat and shoes, I volunteered for 12 months' work with the bomb disposal squad, digging up craters in Liverpool and Bristol.

I got 12 shillings a week – real money in those days. I also signed for the St Helens Town football club as a goalkeeper. There were no wages but they used to pay my bus fares to the games.

A week before Christmas 1948 I was given a month's leave to return to Germany to see my parents. I had been playing for St Helens for only six months but the locals organised a send-off for me at a café in the town.

These people were poor local folk but they said: "We know you're going home and we know the situation in Germany. Here's a little present for you." It was a huge crate filled with blankets, clothes, bacon, butter, sugar, cakes and all kinds of food. There was also an envelope with £150 in it, a fortune at the time.

All this was done out of pure compassion. The Germans were their old enemies yet they appreciated how they had suffered. In my 20 years in Britain I was named Footballer of the Year, I was called the best goalkeeper in the world for 10 years, but that gift in a café in St Helens meant more to me than anything else.

I stayed with St Helens Town FC for as long as I could. But eventually I was talent-spotted by a scout from Manchester City and signed for them in 1949. I got £10 a week in the playing season and £8 in the closed season. I played two Cup Finals at Wembley, both watched by my mother.

But of course the one that gave her the most worry was the 1956 game against Birmingham City.

With 17 minutes of the match remaining, I dived to snatch the ball from the feet of striker Peter Murphy and was knocked unconscious, still clutching the ball. [...]

Bert Trautmann continued to play to the end of the match, which was won by Manchester City 3–0, in spite of a broken vertebra; substitutes were not allowed at the time. In 1956 he was the first foreign player to gain the title of Footballer of the Year. He ended his playing career in 1964 with a farewell match watched by 60,000 supporters. He became a trainer and then ambassador for German football throughout the world. In 2004 he set up the Trautmann Foundation to further Anglo-British understanding through football. In that year he was awarded the Order of the British Empire by Queen Elizabeth II. He now lives near Valencia in Spain.

Vocabulary

1 chant (n.): words or phrases that are repeated by a group of people - **2 goalie** (n.): (infml.) goalkeeper - **17 innocently** (adv.): being done without intending harm to anyone - **26 paratrooper** (n.): a soldier who is trained to jump out of an aircraft with a parachute - **27 to draft** (v.): here: to order s.o. to go to a place by the armed forces - **28 elation** (n.): a feeling of great happines and excitement - **28 triumphalism** (n.): being too proud of your success and too pleased with the defeat of your enemies - **34 to counter** (v.): to do s.th. in order to prevent s.th. bad from happening - **41 to scale** (v.): to climb to the top of s.th. - **52 release** (n.): when s.o. is officially allowed to go free after being kept s.where - **78 send-off** (n.): (infml.) a party when people meet to say goodbye to s.o. who is leaving - **85 compassion** (n.): a strong feeling of sympathy for s.o. who is suffering and a desire to help them - **86 to appreciate** (v.): here: to understand - **92 to talent-spot** (v.): to look for and find young people who are good at sport, music, etc. - **92 scout** (n.): s.o. whose job is to look for young people who are good at sport, music, etc. - **100 striker** (n.): a player in football whose job is to score goals - **101 to clutch** (v.): to hold s.th. tightly because you do not want to lose it

Explanations

5 Manchester City: the smaller and less famous of the two Manchester football clubs, the other being Manchester United - **9 OBE:** Order of the British Empire - **19 Falcons:** English translation of Falken, the youth organisation of the German Social Democratic Party - **21 Jungvolk:** from 1933–45 the part of the Hitler Youth for boys between the ages of 10 and 14 - **34 D-Day landings:** the invasion of German-occupied Europe by Allied forces in Normandy, starting on 4 June, 1944 - **35 Arnhem:** a town in the eastern Netherlands - **35 Ardennes:** a forested hilly region in south-east Belgium, which was the scene of fierce fighting in December 1944 between German and Allied forces. - **37 GI:** a private soldier in the US army; the term originated in the 1930s when it referred to equipment supplied to US forces and was the abbreviation for government issue.- **48 PoW:** short for prisoner of war - **49 Ashton-in-Makerfield:** small town in northwest England - **67 allied raids:** attacks by British and American bombers - **69 bomb disposal squad:** groups of men who deal with bombs which have not exploded and make them safe - **77 St Helens:** town in the county of Lancashire - **95 Cup Final:** the Football Association Cup Final is the match between the two best English football teams - **95 Wembley:** a sports stadium in northwest London where the Cup Final is played

AWARENESS
1 Find out about sportsmen and women who have moved from one European country to another and discuss their possible problems and successes.

COMPREHENSION
2 Write a brief chronology of Bert Trautmann's life as presented in the article.
3 Why was Bert Trautmann put in a special section of the prisoner of war camp for Nazis?
4 Why does the writer put the word "education" (l. 54) in inverted commas?
5 Why did Bert Trautmann stay in England rather than return to Germany?

ANALYSIS
6 Write a character study of Bert Trautmann giving your impression of what kind of person he is and how he developed through his life. Base your answer only on what is written in the article.

OPINION

7 Speculate on why the English people he came into contact with treated Bert Trautmann so well.
8 Why do you think Bert Trautmann said that "that gift in a café in St Helens meant more to me than anything else." (ll. 89f.)?

PROJECT

9 Write a letter to the Trautmann Foundation with a concrete suggestion for a project designed to improve Anglo-German relations among young people.
10 Find out as much as you can about Bert Trautmann in the Internet and write a short biography of him, adding to what you have learnt in the article.

10 John King

The Football Hooligan*

One of England's most notorious exports to Europe is the football hooligan and throughout Europe young men copy his violence, racism, clothing and hairstyles. In some parts of central and eastern Europe hooligans even wave the Union flag as a sign of their allegiance to this cause. In this extract from the last novel in John King's trilogy which explores the mentality of football hooligans, we gain some insight into one hooligan's experience of the ultimate football confrontation: England versus Germany. Tom Johnson has gone to Germany for an England – Germany international soccer game. He and his fellow hooligans are sitting in a bar in Nuremberg talking to some young German football fans. – John King, *England Away* (London: Vintage, 1999), pp. 236ff.

British police deal with football hooligans

1 I nod and have another drink and let Blighty and Harris lead the conversation, looking round at the men drinking and laughing, and there's
5 quite a few with their hair grown out and a couple with flat tops, and there's this little geezer, a real wide-boy with a jack-in-the-box manner, explaining to Mark how the Europeans look at
10 the English hooligans, that whatever they say and do to us, deep down they respect England for the trouble we've caused through the years. Whatever happens, England is the role model
15 for football hooligans. They can't get over these mobs of barbarians who come over and raid their cities, pillaging but not raping, smashing up their shopping centres and causing
20 havoc against the odds. Doesn't matter whether they come from London, Birmingham, Leeds, Newcastle, whatever, they're on a different scale that frightens the shit out of the Continentals. He says the English are
25 rebels. Not in their politics but in their young men, the working class who drink and riot, it's part of the Saxon nature to get pissed and have a laugh, and if anyone starts on them give them a kicking.

Have to admit this bloke knows what he's on about and 30 he's not saying this like he's trying to lick anyone's arse. Has a feel about him that tells you he's dangerous. He knows we're Chelsea and says Chelsea have a cult support, a rebel following, and that the fans have made the club famous through the years. That the Europeans always talk about Chelsea with respect, whether it's Scandinavia, Germany, Croatia. He doesn't know about the Italians and Spanish because they're another set of people, fucking subhumans, and he starts going on about how Western Europe is split between the Saxons and the Latins, that the Germans and the English share the same blood and that it was a tragedy how we fought each other during the war. With the English fighting next to the Germans, the Russians would have been annihilated, the Slavs working for their masters in the West. France wants to be Latin, but can't pull it off, though there's no way you can connect the French and the English or the French and Germans. Everyone does the French.

I think of the game in Paris and the French riot police were firing tear gas as the English gave a mob of French skinheads the run-around. I laugh out loud remembering Rod trying to piss on the eternal flame and wipe out their memories before he was nicked. Mark and the nutter look at me and another German leans in and says his grandfather died fighting the English. I don't know if he wants to have a go or what, but then he says it's stupid this was allowed to happen – friends fighting among themselves when there are better enemies to join forces against. We all nod because there's logic in that, what's the point of killing each other, and I'm off thinking of Vince Matthews and the stories he told us once about the World Cup in 1982 and how the Spanish riot police were always after the English, the police and local fascists both thinking along similar lines, cornering small groups of English when they had the numbers, and how the English were always up for it. The Spanish went for the race connection because we'd given the Argies a good kicking in the Falklands, and when England played Argentina in Mexico a few years later, when Maradona punched the ball over Shilton, the English boys mobbed up outside waiting for the Argies who bottled out, but even so, I don't know about the English and the Germans joining up because I hate the idea of European union. We have to keep ourselves separate, have a drink but go our own ways. I want to tell Hans or whatever the bloke's called that the English don't kill women and kids in concentration camps, no fucking way. It's an essential difference. I know it's not a good idea right now but I can feel the words forming, wondering if I should mention the bombing of London and the plans the Nazis had at the end of the war to execute English prisoners of war, and if that had happened I doubt we'd be sitting here now.

Vocabulary

Intro: notorious (adj.): famous for s.th. bad - **Intro: allegiance** (n.): loyalty to a belief, leader, country, etc. - **5 grown out** (adj.): (of a very short haircut) grown longer - **6 flat top** (n.): a type of hairstyle that is very short and looks flat on top - **7 geezer** (n.): (infml.) man - **7 wide-boy** (n.): (infml.) here: a man or youth who you cannot trust - **8 jack-in-the-box** (adj.): making sudden and unexpected movements - **14 role model** (n.): s.o. whose behaviour people try to copy because they admire them - **15f. to get over s.th.** (v.): to successfully deal with a problem or difficulty - **17 to raid** (v.): to make a sudden attack on a place - **18 to pillage** (v.): to steal a lot of things and do a lot of damage - **18 to rape** (v.): to force s.o. to have sex - **20 havoc** (n.): a situation in which there is a lot of damage or lack of order - **20 against the odds** (adv.): here: in spite of greater numbers of people against you - **23 whatever** (adv.): here: it doesn't matter where - **23 scale** (n.): here: level of activity that is happening - **24 Continentals** (n.): people who live in Europe, not including Britain - **26 to riot** (v.): (of a crowd) to behave in a violent and uncontrolled way - **26 Saxon** (adj.): belonging to a member of the group of people who lived in northern Europe, some of whom came to Britain in the 5th century - **27 to get pissed** (v.): (slang) to get drunk - **27 to have a laugh** (v.): to have fun and enjoy yourself - **28 to start on s.o.**: (infml.) to annoy s.o.- **29 bloke** (n.): (infml.) man - **29 to be on about s.th.** (v.): (infml.) here: to talk about s.th. - **38 fucking** (adj.): (taboo) here: used to emphasise your opinion of s.th. - **38 to go on about** (v.): (infml.) to talk for a long time about s.th. - **43 to annihilate** (v.): to destroy s.th. or s.o. completely - **45 to pull s.th. off** (v.): (infml.) to do s.th. successfully - **47 to do s.o.** (v.): here: to attack, criticise - **49f. to give s.o. the run-around** (v.): (infml.) here: to give s.o. a lot of trouble - **52 to wipe out** (v.): to destroy s.th. completely - **52 to nick s.o.** (v.): (infml.) if the police nick you, they catch you and charge you with a crime - **53 nutter** (n.): (infml.) a crazy person, an idiot - **55 to have a go** (v.): (infml.) to have a fight - **58 to join forces** (v.): to do s.th. together with other people - **60 to be off** (v.): (infml.) to no longer pay attention to s.th. - **63f. to think along similar lines** (v.): to have similar opinions - **64 to corner** (v.): to force a person into a position from which they cannot escape - **65f. to be up for s.th.** (v.): (infml.) to be prepared, ready for s.th. - **70 to mob up** (v.): (infml.) to gather in a crowd - **71 to bottle out** (v.): (infml.) to suddenly decide not to do s.th. because you are frightened

Explanations

Intro: Nuremberg: English for Nürnberg - **32 Chelsea:** Chelsea Football Club with its stadium at Stamford Bridge in west London - **40 Latins:** peoples from southern Europe whose languages developed from Latin: Spain. Portugal, Italy, France - **44 Slavs:** people from central and eastern Europe who speak Slavic languages such as Russian, Polish, Czech, Bulgarian - **51 eternal flame:** the flame which burns under the archway of the Arc de Triomphe in Paris; it has burned continuously since 1921 and commemorates the French dead of two world wars who were not identified - **67 Argies:** Argentinians - **68 Falklands:** Falkland Islands; islands in the South Atlantic about 500 km off the coast of Argentina; they have been a British colony since 1832. In 1982 Argentinian forces invaded the islands and in the war with Britain that resulted from this Argentina was defeated and the islands became British colonies again. - **77 no fucking way:** (taboo) used to say that you will definitely not do or allow s.th.

AWARENESS
1. What do you think motivates the behaviour of football hooligans?

COMPREHENSION
2. Why, according to the narrator, are English football hooligans admired on the Continent?
3. Why does the narrator add the proviso "not in their politics" (l. 25) to the statement that the English are rebels?

ANALYSIS
4. Show how the narrator confuses the concepts "race", "culture" and "language". Make sure you define these terms carefully.
5. Analyse the author's use of the first-person narrator technique.

OPINION
6. Give your own personal assessment of the character of the narrator.
7. What are the arguments for and against writing about such characters as a football hooligan in fiction?

PROJECTS
8. Investigate the history of football hooliganism in England.
9. Compare the first-person narration in *England Away* with another first-person novel you know.

11 "We want to be loved by you ..."

The 2006 World Cup in Germany gave the British press an opportunity to analyse and discuss Anglo-German relations. In this article Richard Johnson describes his conversations with German passengers on the train from Hamburg to Berlin and then with German journalists and politicians. – *The Sunday Times Magazine*, 28 May 2006, pp. 41–43.

The Inter City Express from Hamburg to Berlin has recycling bins, and Wi-Fi, and self-cleaning toilets. But it's still a minute late leaving the *Hauptbahnhof*. Since trains and punctuality are so important in the German world, the Deutsche Bahn hands out official certificates of train tardiness (*Bescheinigung über Zugverspätung*) if a train is late. A minute doesn't count as Zugverspätung, not even in Germany, but you can use the certificates as an official explanation of why you're late for work or school. Or keep them as a souvenir of living the German way. My guidebook says, to greet strangers in Germany, simply knock twice on the table. It means: "Hello, everyone." I try it, but everyone on the train turns round to find out what all the knocking is about. I figure my guidebook is out of date and try another approach, "Hello, jeder," I say. Everyone looks surprised at an Englishman speaking German. As one man says, "We have a joke in Germany: if you speak three languages, you're trilingual. If you speak two languages, you're bilingual. If you speak one, you're English."

The conversation is hesitant at first – like my German. So we start to talk about Anglo-German relations in English. The Germans will speak English at any opportunity. There are about 450 English words in the German vocabulary. They use them as often as possible mainly to prove how sophisticated and educated they are. Many English verbs are "Germanised" and absorbed into the language – for instance, "managen", "involvieren", "e-mailen" – and it doesn't seem to create a scandal the way it does in France.

Talk on the train is in "Denglish" – that wonderful mix of Deutsch and English, such as: "Hello, Sir! How goes it you?"

"Oh, thank you for the afterquestion."

"Are you already long here?"

"No, first a pair days. I am not out London."

"Will we now drink a beer? My throat is outdried."

But there's nothing self-conscious about it: they are just happy to practise their language skills. They dislike the undemocratic concept of private hospitals or public schools. But they talk, openly, about needing a German Margaret Thatcher to deal with the country's unions. They declare undying devotion to the German republic but, secretly, they love our monarchy. It represents continuity to a country full of discontinuity. They loved Princess Diana (or "Lady Dee", as one passenger calls her), and German TV still screens the "Queen's Birthday Parade" (Trooping the Colour) every June.

When the train pulls into Berlin Zoo, the station newsstands are full of one story. A picture of the chancellor, Angela Merkel, in her swimsuit appeared in *The Sun* – under the headline "I'm Big in the Bumdestag" – and the German press are furious. "You are rotten to the core," says the Bild-Zeitung columnist Franz Josef Wagner. In Britain the picture was accompanied by stories about Germany's much-improved "bottom line", but in Germany it has been seen as something else. An act of gross disrespect. As Wagner writes, "Where does this hatred come from?"

Germany' ex-minister of culture, Michael Naumann, experienced the hatred of the British newspapers first-hand. His comment in an interview about Anglo-German relations ("There is no other country in Europe that hinges [its] identity as strongly as Great Britain does on the second world war. And she has every right to do so") was badly edited – the second sentence was missed out. "But my German sense of humour failed utterly when the paper followed up with the headline 'That is why we won't forget, Herr Minister!' showing a picture of Bergen-Belsen." Naumann insists he doesn't need a lesson on the Holocaust – his Jewish relatives, who barely escaped the Third Reich, returned to Germany in British and American uniforms. And he doesn't need a lesson in the ways of the British – he counts his time at Queen's College, Oxford, as the happiest of his life: "I enjoyed the absence of the bureaucracy," he says, "and a generally highly cultured tone of political discussion, much more tolerant of other people's views than over here in Germany."

Dr Ulf Poschardt, political columnist for *Die Welt*, has suggested we talk about Anglo-German relations over tea. Germans think we still drink afternoon tea. Heidi Klum, married to an Englishman – the singer Seal – is in full agreement: "What can I say? My husband shows me how to make a good cuppa. And as for 'No sex please, we're British,' it just doesn't apply." The English-language textbooks in German schools, which now focus on America, last focused on England in the 1960s. So they imagine we are all Miss Marple and "How d'you do?" They take their pronunciation from the same books, which is why Germans still pronounce the A as E. At McDonalds, a German will order a Big Mec and say "Thenk you," [...]

Poschardt studies the film *Notting Hill* to improve his English, and his diction has a Hugh Grant quality about it: his friends call him "Posh". His tailoring is bespoke, and he drinks sparkling water with lemon. Recently he wrote a column for *Die Welt* from a wooden bench on Hampstead Heath. "The bench was inscribed 'in loving memory of Sarah' and nobody tried to deface it," he said. "Everybody respected it, no matter what their culture or background was. I thought that was a miracle. In Germany someone would have drawn a swastika or a penis on it."

But in other ways Germany is more respectful than Britain. Politicians' private lives are strictly off limits. And so is Angela Merkel's bottom. Poschardt says educated Germans completely understand the humour of our tabloid headlines, "but there's no such culture in the tabloids here in Germany. And because of our history, we don't offend other countries like that. Or put them down. The only people we put down are anti-Israel. And pro-fascist."

[...]

The Germans think British tabloids reflect our arrogance. [Matthias] Matussek reckons we've got more arrogant since the British economy improved – and the German economy stagnated: "The best way to improve your image with us is to lose your money. If we want to cheer ourselves up, we look at your NHS.

English fans say "Thank you" to Germany for the World Championship 2006 before the England vs Germany match on 22 August 2007 in Wembley stadium

And your education. But give us something to laugh about, for goodness' sake. How about a recession, or Beckham hitting the bar during a penalty shoot-out against the Germans? Or worst of all, Bridget Jones Part III."

When he was the London correspondent for *Der Spiegel*, Matussek enjoyed dinners with leading British intellectuals. But one in particular – with AS Byatt – sticks in his mind. "Over dessert, she asked me for my opinion on the European constitution. I said, 'It's interesting – I think all states should agree on common principles. What about you?' 'Well,' she said, 'we British are the oldest democracy in the world. We don't need constitutions. But for young nations like yours it might be very helpful.' I could have killed her. So arrogant."

[...]

Vocabulary

6 tardiness (n.): arriving late – **15 to figure** (v.): here: think – **27 sophisticated** (adj.): having a lot of experience of life – **29 to absorb** (v.): here: to become part of s.th. larger – **39 self-conscious** (adj.): worried and embarrassed about what other people think of you – **46 devotion** (n.): strong love for s.th. or s.o. – **55 to screen** (v.): to show a film or television programme – **67 columnist** (n.): s.o. who writes articles that appear regularly in a newspaper – **71 gross** (adj.): wrong and unacceptable – **77 to hinge** (v.): /hɪndʒ/ to depend – **79 to edit** (v.): to prepare for printing by deciding what to include – **81 utterly** (adv.): completely – **109 tailoring** (n.): the way a man's clothes are made – **109 posh** (adj.): upper class – **110 bespoke** (adj.): made specially for a particular customer – **111 column** (n.): an article on a particular topic or by a particular journalist that appears regularly in a nespaper – **114 to deface** (v.): to spoil the appearance of s.th. – **117 swastika** (n.): the symbol of the Nazi Party – **119 off limits** (adj.): taboo – **120 bottom** (n.): the part of your body that you sit on – **122 tabloid** (n.): belonging to a newspaper that has small pages, a lot of photographs and stories mainly about sex and famous people etc., rather than serious news – **125 to put down** (v.): to criticise s.o. and make them feel stupid – **129 to reckon** (v.): to think – **136 bar** (n.): the long piece of wood across the top of a goal

Explanations

2 Wi-Fi: also wi-fi; abbreviation of wireless fidelity, a way of connecting computers to a network by using radio signals rather than wires – **42 public school:** a private school for children between 13 and 18, whose parents pay for their education – **65f. Bumdestag:** word play combining the word bum for bottom and Bundestag; this kind of word play is typical of British tabloid newspapers – **67 rotten to the core:** completely bad – **68 Franz Josef Wagner:** (b. 1943) conservative German journalist – **70 bottom line:** word play combining the two meanings of the phrase "bottom line": one meaning the shape of your bottom, the other mean the most important thing to be considered – **73 Michael Naumann:** (b. 1941) German politician and journalist – **83 Bergen-Belsen:** concentration camp and prisoner of war camp mainly for prisoners from the Soviet Union situated about sixty km northeast of Hanover – **84 Holocaust:** the killing of millions of Jews and other people by the Nazis during the Second World War – **88 Queen's College:** one of the oldest colleges forming part of Oxford University – **93 Die Welt:** daily newspaper, generally considered to be conservative – **95 afternoon tea:** a small meal of cake or biscuits eaten in the afternoon with a cup of tea – **96 Heidi Klum:** (b. 1973) German model, married to the English singer Seal (Seal Henry Olusegun Olumide Adelo Samuel) – **97 Seal:** (b. 1963) English singer of Nigerian and Brazilian ancestry, (for full name see: Heidi Klum) born in London – **98 cuppa:** (spoken) cup of tea – **99 No sex please, we're British:** the title of a farce first staged in London in 1971 and later turned into a film in 1973. The title has become a standard quotation or catch phrase. – **102 Miss Marple:** a detective character created by the English writer Agatha Christie (1890-1976) – **103 "How d'you do?":** Many foreigners mistakenly think this is the way British people usually greet each other. – **105 A as E:** The author, like many British visitors to Germany, thinks that the German mispronunciation of A as E, as in "Big Mec" is a result of old-fashioned pronunciation taught in German schools. They think that German teachers learned their English from teachers who learned their English in the 1930s when this pronunciation was popular among upper-class English speakers. A more probable explanation is that the sound /æ/ as represented by the letter A is simply missing in German. German speakers transfer the /æ/ sound to the nearest German equivalent which is /e/. – **107 Notting Hill:** a romantic comedy starring Hugh Grant and Julia Roberts, which takes place in the Notting Hill district of London – **108 Hugh Grant:** (b. 1969) English actor, born in London; He is considered by many people to represent in manner, speech and appearance the "typical" upper-class Englishman. – **110 sparkling water:** water with carbon dioxide in it – **112 Hampstead Heath:** a large area of open park and woodland four miles north of the centre of London – **129 Matthias Matussek:** (b. 1954) German journalist who now writes for *Der Spiegel*. He was *Der Spiegel* correspondent in London. – **133 NHS:** the National Health Service; founded in 1948, it provides medical care for everyone and is paid for out of taxes and national insurance. – **136 Beckham:** (b. 1975) David, English footballer, born in London, has played for Manchester United, Real Madrid and for the English national team. – **136 penalty shoot-out:** a situation when each team in a football match takes penalty kicks (one player from one team tries to kick the ball into the goal of the other team) as a way of deciding which team will win when the ordinary part of the match has ended with both teams having the same number of goals or not having got any goals – **137 Bridget Jones:** a young single woman who is the central character in two films, *Bridget Jones's Diary* (2001) and *Bridget Jones: The Edge of Reason* (2004). The two films are based on novels of the same name by Helen Fielding which are in turn based on a newspaper column written by Helen Fielding for the *Independent* newspaper. – **141f. A S Byatt:** (b. 1936) (Antonia, Susan) English writer, broadcaster, critic, born in Yorkshire, sister of the writer Margaret Drabble

Awareness

1. Discuss what you think are the main differences between life in Britain and Germany under the headings: social behaviour, daily life, food and drink, and education. State what evidence you base your opinions on – personal experience, friends' experience, the media, school and schoolbooks, hearsay.

Comprehension

2. Translate the "Denglish" conversation (ll. 33 ff.) into real English and real German.
3. What do the Germans mentioned in the article especially like and dislike about Britain?

Analysis

4. What is the function of the description of the train in the first six lines?
5. Explain what Richard Johnson does wrong when he tries to communicate with the other German passengers and describe what he should have done.
6. What are the differences in German and British attitudes towards politicians mentioned in the article?
7. Summarise the impression of Germans and Germany that Richard Johnson gives to his readers and explain the means he uses to create this impression.

Opinion

8. Explain why you agree or disagree with the comment that Germans use English words "as often as possible mainly to prove how sophisticated and educated they are." (ll. 26 ff.)
9. "You are rotten to the core" (ll. 66 f.) Write a polemical essay in which you either criticise or defend Franz Josef Wagner's attack on the British press's treatment of Angela Merkel.
10. Write a letter to Richard Johnson in which you give your opinion on what he has written about Germans and Germany and make suggestions as to how he could have given a truer and fairer impression of the German people and of German life.

Internet Project

11. In the Internet look up articles by Franz Josef Wagner and Matthias Matussek on Britain and the British press. Discuss how fairly they deal with the topic of Anglo-German relations.

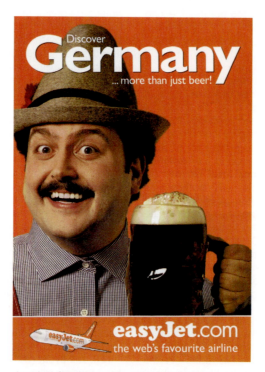

A typical German – according to EasyJet

12 Winston Churchill

1946 – Winston Churchill calls for a United States of Europe*

On 19 September 1946, just over one year after the end of the Second World War, Winston Churchill gave a remarkable speech at Zurich University. It was remarkable on three counts: it advocated a "United States of Europe"; at its core would be Franco-German reconciliation; and the only role he saw for Britain in this enterprise was as a "sponsor". – (www.ena.lu/europe/pioneering/speech-winston-churchill-zurich-1946.htm)

Mr President, Ladies and Gentlemen,

I am honoured today by being received in your ancient university and by the address which has been given to me on your behalf and which I greatly value.

I wish to speak to you today about the tragedy of Europe. This noble continent, comprising on the whole the fairest and most cultivated regions of the earth, enjoying a temperate and equable climate, is the home of all the great parent races of the western world. It is the fountain of Christian faith and Christian ethics. It is the origin of most of the culture, the arts, philosophy and science both of ancient and modern times. If Europe were once united in the sharing of its common inheritance, there would be no limit to the happiness, to the prosperity and the glory which its three or four hundred million people would enjoy. Yet it is from Europe that have sprung that series of frightful nationalistic quarrels, originated by the Teutonic nations in their rise to power, which we have seen in the twentieth century and even in our own lifetime, wreck the peace and mar the prospects of all mankind.

And what is the plight to which Europe has been reduced? Some of the smaller states have indeed made a good recovery, but over wide areas a vast quivering mass of tormented, hungry, care-worn and bewildered human beings gape at the ruins of their cities and their homes, and scan the dark horizons for the approach of some new peril, tyranny or terror. Among the victors there is a babel of voices; among the vanquished the sullen silence of despair. That is all that Europeans, grouped in so many ancient states and nations, that is all that the Germanic races have got by tearing each other to pieces and spreading havoc far and wide.

Winston Churchill giving his speech at Zurich University in 1946

Indeed but for the fact that the great Republic across the Atlantic Ocean has at length realised that the ruin or enslavement of Europe would involve their own fate as well, and has stretched out hands of succour and of guidance, but for that the Dark Ages would have returned in all their cruelty and squalor. Gentlemen, they may still return.

Yet all the while there is a remedy which, if it were generally and spontaneously adopted by the great majority of people in many lands, would as if by a miracle transform the whole scene, and would in a few years make all Europe, or the greater part of it, as free and as happy as Switzerland is today. What is this sovereign remedy? It is to recreate the European family, or as much of it as we can, and to provide it with a structure under which it can dwell in peace, in safety and in freedom. We must build a kind of United States of Europe. In this way only will hundreds of millions of toilers be able to regain the simple joys and hopes which make life worth living. The process is simple. All that is needed is the resolve of hundreds of millions of men and women to do right instead of wrong and to gain as their reward blessing instead of cursing.

[...]

I am going to say something that will astonish you. The first step in the recreation of the European Family must be a partnership between France and Germany. In this way only can France recover the moral and cultural leadership of Europe. There can be no revival of Europe without a spiritually great France and a spiritually great Germany. The structure of the United States of Europe, if well and truly built, will be such as to make the material strength of a single state less important. Small nations will count as much as large ones and gain their honour by their contribution to the common cause. The ancient states and principalities of Germany, freely joined together for mutual convenience in a federal system, might take their individual places among the United States of Europe. I shall not try to make a detailed programme for hundreds of millions of people who want to be happy and free, prosperous and safe, who wish to enjoy the four freedoms of which the great President Roosevelt spoke, and live in accordance with the principles embodied in the Atlantic Charter.

If this is their wish, if this is the wish of the Europeans in so many lands, they have only to say so, and means can certainly be found, and the machinery erected, to carry that wish to full fruition.

[...]

I must now sum up the propositions which are before you. Our constant aim must be to build and fortify the strength of the United Nations Organization. Under and within that world concept we must recreate the European Family in a regional structure called, it may be, the United States of Europe. And the first practical step would be to form a Council of Europe. If at times all the states of Europe are not willing or able to join the Union, we must nevertheless proceed to assemble and combine those who will and those who can. The salvation of the common people of every race and of every land from war or servitude must be established on solid foundations and must be guarded by the readiness of all men and women to die rather than submit to tyranny. In all this urgent work, France and Germany must take the lead together. Great Britain, the British Commonwealth of Nations, mighty America and I trust Soviet Russia – for then indeed all would be well – must be the friends and sponsors of the new Europe and must champion its right to live and shine.

Therefore I say to you: let Europe arise!

Vocabulary

Intro: reconciliation (n.): here: a situation in which two countries become friendly with each other again after a war – **6 address** (n.): fml. speech made to a group of people – **16 fair** (adj.): (archaic) beautiful, attractive – **17 cultivated** (adj.): intelligent and knowing a lot about art, literature and music – **19 temperate** (adj.): not very hot or very cold – **20 equable** (adj.): not varying very much between hot and cold – **21 fountain** (n.): here: place where you get s.th. from – **25 inheritance** (n.): ideas, skills, literature from the past that influence people in the present – **30 to originate** (v.): to come from a particular place – **30 Teutonic** (adj.): here: relating to Germany and Austria – **32 to mar** (v.): to spoil, make s.th. less pleasant – **33 prospects** (n.): chances of future success – **34 plight** (n.): a very bad situation – **36 quivering** (adj.): here: shaking, trembling because you are very afraid – **37 tormented** (adj.): suffering extreme mental and physical pain – **37 care-worn** (adj.): looking sad, worried and tired – **37 bewildered** (adj): totally confused – **38 to gape** (v.): to look at s.th. for a long time, esp. with your mouth open – **39 to scan** (v.): to examine an area carefully but quickly – **40 peril** (n.): great danger – **41 vanquished** (n.): here: the people who have lost a war – **42 sullen** (adj.): angry and silent – **44 Germanic** (adj.): here: relating to Germany and Austria – **46 havoc** (n.): a situation in which there is a lot of damage or lack of order – **57 succour** (n.): /ˈsʌkə/ help that is given to s.o. – **58 guidance** (n.): help and advice that is given to s.o. – **62 squalor** (n.): /ˈskwɒlə/ the condition of being dirty because of a lack of care or money – **64 remedy** (n.): a way of dealing with a problem or making a bad situation better – **70 sovereign** (adj.): /ˈsɒvrɪn/ here: best – **72 to dwell** (v.): to live – **75 toiler** (n.): s.o. who works very hard – **77 resolve** (n.): strong determination to succeed – **79 blessing** (n.): s.th. that happens to which is good, s.o.'s encouragement for what you do – **79 cursing** (n.): s.o. telling you that what you do is bad, words that that you say because you are angry – **85 revival** (n.): a process in which s.th. becomes active or strong again – **91 common cause** (n): an aim or activity you share with other people – **92 principality** (n.): a country that is ruled by a prince – **93 mutual convenience** (n.): here: s.th. which is important for both groups of people – **99 embodied** (adj.): contained, included – **103 to erect** (v.): to build, construct s.th. – **104 fruition** (n.): if a wish or plan is carried to fruition, it is successfully put into action and completed – **106 proposition** (n.): offer, suggestion – **107 to fortify** (v.): to make stronger – **114 nevertheless** (adv.): in spite of a fact that you have just mentioned – **116 salvation** (n.): s.th. that saves s.o. from danger – **117 servitude** (n.): the condition of being a slave – **119 to submit** (v.): to agree to obey

Explanations

21 parent races: one can only speculate on the meaning of this vague phrase. "Parent" implies "ancestor", "educator", and "controller"; see task 8 below. – **30 Teutonic nations:** Germany and Austria – **49 the great Republic:** the United States of America – **59 Dark Ages:** AD 476–1000 – **97f. four freedoms:** freedom from war; freedom from want and fear; freedom of self-determination; freedom of trade – **98 President Roosevelt:** (Franklin Delano, 1882–1945) the 32nd president of the United States, served four terms (1932–1945) – **100 Atlantic Charter:** the Atlantic Charter was negotiated by the British prime minister Winston Churchill and the American president Franklin D. Roosevelt aboard warships anchored off Newfoundland in August 1941. The main points of the charter were: 1) no territorial gains sought by the United States or the United Kingdom; 2) changes in national territory only in accordance with the wishes of the peoples concerned; 3) the right of self-determination of peoples; 4) trade barriers to be lowered; 5) global economic co-operation and advancement of social welfare; 6) freedom from want and fear; 7) freedom of the seas; 8) disarmament of aggressor nations, post-war common disarmament. – **112 Council of Europe:** an association of European states founded in 1949 to promote economic and social co-operation – **121f. British Commonwealth of Nations:** now called the Commonwealth of Nations or just Commonwealth; it consists of the UK and states that were previously part of the British Empire. The British monarch is its symbolic head. – **123 Soviet Russia:** Soviet Union, full name Union of Soviet Socialist Republics or USSR

AWARENESS
1 What do you know about Winston Churchill: his family, his political career, and his time as prime minister of Britain during the Second World War?

COMPREHENSION
2 What does Churchill mean by "that series of frightful nationalistic quarrels originated by the Teutonic nations ..." (ll. 29f.)?
3 Who is Churchill referring to when he speaks of "a vast quivering mass of tormented hungry care-worn and bewildered human beings ..." (ll. 36ff.)?
4 In what ways did the United States stretch out "hands of succour and of guidance" (ll. 57f.) to Europe after World War II?
5 Why was Switzerland so "free and [...] happy" (l. 68f.) in comparison with the rest of Europe?
6 Why did Churchill expect his demand that "The first step in the recreation of the European family must be a partnership between France and Germany" (l. 82f.) would astonish his audience?

ANALYSIS
7 Analyse Churchill's speech considering what he says, the way he says it and the effect he wishes to have on his audience. Pay careful attention to the terms in which he describes Europe's past, present and future.

OPINION
8 Discuss Churchill's contention that Europe is a) "the home of all the great parent races of the western world" (ll. 19f.) and b) "the origin of most of the culture, arts, philosophy and science of ancient and modern times" (ll. 22ff.). Try to define what he might mean by "parent races" (l. 21).
9 Do you think that Churchill is being fair when he says that the frightful nationalistic quarrels in the twentieth century "originated by the Teutonic nations in their rise to power" (ll. 30f.)?
10 Write a report giving your opinion of Churchill's speech and your personal reaction to his language, opinions, and ideas.

PROJECT
11 Write a chronology of the European Union from its founding as the European Economic Community to the present day.

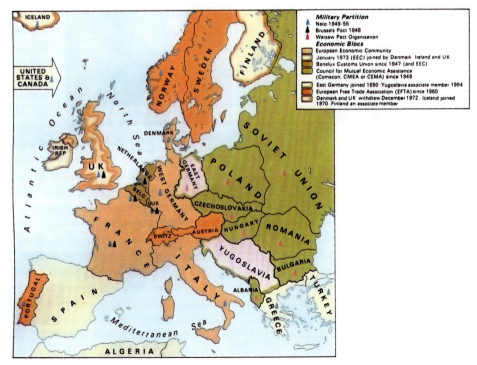

The Times Atlas of World History (ed. Geoffrey Barraclough), London: Times Books, 1980, p. 274

13 Timothy Garton Ash

Janus Britain*

Like many European countries Britain has two faces, one pointing towards Europe and one away from it. In this extract from his book *Free World* Timothy Garton Ash shows that, in fact, Britain has four faces, all pointing in different directions. Britain's complex position in the modern world is made clear by a walk down the high street of a London suburb. – Timothy Garton Ash, *Free World* (London: Penguin Books, 2005), pp. 15–18.

If you take the Number 74 red double-decker bus from Baker Street you will eventually cross the River Thames at Putney. On the south bank of the river, immediately to your left as you come across Putney Bridge, you will spy a church, half-hidden among the trees. Most of your fellow passengers – their faces set in the tired, closed mask of the London commuter – will not spare it a glance. Yet in this Church of St Mary the Virgin, on 29 October 1647, one Thomas Rainsborough spoke words that have resounded through the modern history of the West.

At the height of the English Civil War, England's revolutionary army was debating who should have the vote in elections to the Westminster parliament. Radical 'Levellers' among the officers and regimental delegates were locked in fierce dispute with Oliver Cromwell. According to notes made at the time, Colonel Rainsborough said:

For really I think that the poorest he that is in England hath a life to live, as the greatest he; and therefore truly, sir, I think it's very clear, that every man that is to live under a government ought first by his own consent to put himself under that government; and I do think that the poorest man in England is not at all bound in a strict sense to that government that he hath not had a voice to put himself under.

The poorest she still did not get a look in, but this was nevertheless a revolutionary statement of the claim for government by consent and equal political rights for all citizens. Here in Putney, in 1647, a plainspoken English gentleman demanded and described the essence of what we mean today when we say 'democracy'. His claim echoed around the old world – and into the new. Thomas Rainsborough's sister married John Winthrop, the Puritan governor of Massachussetts Bay Colony who declared that New England should be 'as a City upon a Hill'. His younger brother settled in Boston. There are six towns called Putney in the United States.

[...] Leaving the church and turning left up Putney High Street, this is what you will see: Hot Wok Express, Il Peperone pizzeria, Enoteca (an Italian restaurant), the Odeon cinema (probably showing an American movie), Sydney (an Australian bar-restaurant), La Mancha (a Spanish tapas bar and restaurant), Superdrug, McDonald's and right next to it the coffee place Costa, Caff, Nero [...], Starbucks, United Colors of Benetton, Prêt à Manger, Burger King, Rogiero's café, the Piccolo Bar – and that's only up to the railway station.

Modern shops in Putney High Street

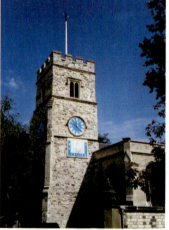

The Church of St Mary the Virgin, Putney

In between are the old sturdy British familiars: Thomas Cook's travel agency, Millets, British Home Stores, the Abbey National building society turned bank, Boots the chemist, Thornton's chocolate shop, the Halifax, W. H. Smith's. Halfway down the high street there is a pub called Ye Olde Spotted Horse, which features, amidst its faux-Elizabethan white-and-black half-timbering, a large and rather handsome nineteenth-century model of a black-and-white dray horse. But the British horse, unlike the leopard, can change his spots. For inside this Victorian pub, blackboards above the bar now offer 'Wines of the Day: Merlot – Chile, Pinot Noir – NZ, Rioja – Spain, Shiraz Cabernet – Australia, Côtes du Rhône – France'. The menu promises 'Linguine with Ham and Goat's Cheese Sauce' and 'Creme de Menthe Ice Cream Bombes'. A Young's Brewery poster on the wall promotes not beer but wine, with this incentive: 'Win a Trip to Spain!'

You may say this is just the superficial, brand-and-chain Americanization and Europeanization that we now encounter everywhere in the developed world; what has been called the Euro-American shopping mall. But the internationalism of Putney goes a lot deeper. Quite a few of the apartments in the riverside block that looms behind the church are rented by city firms for their foreign staff: 'A lot of Yanks,' says Reverend Fraser [of St Mary's Church]. The French community can be met in St Simon's Church in Hazlewell Road, and there was until recently a French bookshop in Lower Richmond Road. Nearby, there's the headquarters of Voluntary Services Overseas, which in 2002 sent some 1,600 British volunteers to work in forty-three developing countries. In Upper Richmond Road you can call on Longview Solutions, a software company promising to provide you with 'a single source of financial truth'. Its other offices are in Toronto, Philadelphia, Chicago, Dallas, San Jose, Atlanta and Madrid.

Everywhere there are what a local estate agent snootily calls 'the Antipodeans'. Australians and New Zealanders – 'thousands of them' cries the estate agent, with a mixture of personal disgust and professional delight – pack into rented accommodation and cram the Sydney bar. No worries. The district of Southfields, a maze of small streets, is now a little South Africa. The local MP quotes an estimate that as many as 20,000 South Africans live there. People from the rest of the Commonwealth – that noble republican moniker of the Cromwellian revolution, now incongruously applied to Her Britannic Majesty's former Empire – from Pakistan, India, Africa and the Caribbean, are not yet so numerous as in neighbouring parts of London. Putney can nevertheless already boast a Sikh temple, an African Families Association, and, in Gressenhall Road, the world headquarters of the Ahmadis, a dissident Muslim sect originating in the Punjab and claiming millions of adherents in seventy countries. Finally, and resented by many local people, who believe they are taking scarce council housing, jobs and benefits, there are the asylum-seekers from every unhappy corner of the world.

What you glimpse here, in Putney, are the many faces of Britain at the beginning of the twenty-first century. Janus, the Roman god of doorways, passages and bridges, had two faces, usually depicted on the front and back of his head, pointing in opposite directions. Janus Britain has four. The back and front faces can be labelled 'Island' and 'World'; the face on the left says 'Europe' and that on the right 'America'. No wonder Britain's head aches.

Old vs. new: a pub and a building society on Putney High Street

Thomas Rainsborough's historic demand for democracy and equal rights at the Church of St Mary the Virgin, Putney

Vocabulary

5 to spy (v.): here: to see – **7 commuter** (n.): s.o. who travels a long distance to work everyday – **8 to spare a glance** (v.): to look quickly at s.o. or s.th. – **10 to resound** (v.): here: to be mentioned or talked about a lot – **33 consent** (n.): agreement – **38 to get a look in** (v.): (infml.) to have a chance to take part in s.th. – **41 plainspoken** (adj.): saying exactly what you think, esp. in a way that people think is honest – **88 bombe** (n.): a frozen round-shaped dessert – **89 incentive** (n.): s.th. that encourages you to start a new activity, try harder, etc. – **97 to loom** (v.): to appear as a large unclear shape – **111 estate agent** (n.): s.o. whose business is to buy and sell houses or land for people – **111 snootily** (adv.): rudely and in an unfriendly way because you think you are better than other people – **115 to cram** (v.): if a lot of people cram a place they fill it – **120 moniker** (n.): (infml.) name – **121 incongruously** (adv.): here: unsuitably – **125 to boast** (v.): if a place boasts s.th. it has s.th. that is very good or special – **129 adherent** (n.): here: s.o. who supports a particular belief – **130 to resent** (v.): to feel angry about a situation because you think it is unfair – **134 to glimpse** (v.): to see s.o. or s.th. for a moment

Explanations

Title: Janus: an old Italian god, the guardian of doorways and gates and protector of the state in times of war. He is usually shown with two faces so that he looks both forwards and backwards. – **2 Baker Street:** a street in the West End of London famous for being the location of the flat of Sherlock Holmes, the fictional detective, at no. 221B – **3 Putney:** district of London south of the River Thames – **8 Church of St Mary the Virgin:** originally built in the 15th century, scene of the Putney Debates in 1647 in the English Civil War when the future of England and its government were discussed – **9 Thomas Rainsborough:** an officer in Oliver Cromwell's revolutionary army and member of the Levellers group, which demanded the vote for all men, equal rights, religious freedom and a reduction in extremes of wealth in society. – **12 English Civil War:** 1642 to 1646, between Charles II and his supporters, the Royalists (or Cavaliers), and the Parliamentarians (or Roundheads). In 1649 Charles was tried and executed; England was a republic, or Commonwealth, from 1649 to 1660. – **25 he:** here: man – **27 as:** archaic for like – **38 she:** here: woman – **45f. John Winthrop:** (1588–1649) born in the county of Suffolk, England; he was a deeply religious man and became dissatisfied with the persecution of the Puritans. In 1629 he decided to go to North America and after being elected governor of the Massechussetts Bay Company, he left aboard the ship Arbella in 1630. – **47f. "as a city upon a hill":** an allusion to Matthew 5:14 ("ye are the light of the world. A city that is set on a hill cannot be hid"). This famous phrase was uttered in Winthrop's sermon "A Modell of Christian Charity" in which he set out the goals of the Puritan mission and the means by which to attain them. (For further details see: Detlef Rediker and Donald Turner (eds.), *Religion in the U.S.A. In God We Trust*, München: Langenscheidt-Longman, 1997.) – **57 Superdrug:** a chain of chemists – **59 Prêt à Manger:** a chain of sandwich bars – **67 Millets:** a chain of shops selling sports and outdoor clothing – **67f. British Home Stores:** a chain of shops selling clothing and food – **70 building society:** a type of bank that you pay money into in order to save it and earn interest and that will lend you money to buy a house or flat – **74f. W. H. Smith's:** a chain of newsagents and bookshops – **78 Ye olde:** an imitation of what is thought to be an old form of English; in fact "ye" is simply an alternative way of writing "the". – **79 faux-Elizabethan:** an imitation of the style of building during the reign of Queen Elizabeth I (1533–1603) – **79 half-timbering:** a style of building popular during the reign of Queen Elizabeth I (1533–1603) in which the wooden structure of the building could be seen on the outside walls – **84 NZ:** New Zealand – **91 brand:** a type of product made by a particular company that has a particular name or design – **98 Yank:** (infml.) American – **103 Voluntary Services Overseas:** a British charity which promotes voluntary work especially by young adults in developing countries – **118 MP:** Member of Parliament – **121 Cromwellian revolution:** Oliver Cromwell (1599-1658) was the leader of the parliamentary forces in the English Civil War (see above) and was head of state, Lord Protector, while England was a republic. This period was called the Commonwealth. – **125 Sikh:** connected with Sikhism, a monotheistic religion founded in Punjab

AWARENESS

1. What are the main relationships that Britain and Germany have with countries outside the European Union?

COMPREHENSION

2. What are the countries, apart from England, that have left their mark on Putney High Street?
3. Which countries have the English of Putney influenced?

ANALYSIS

4. What is so significant for the modern history of the West of Thomas Rainsborough's words (ll. 24 ff.)?
5. What does Putney High Street tell us about modern Britain?
6. Explain the distinction between the "superficial ... Americanization and Europeanization" (ll. 91f.) of Putney and the rest of the world and the "deeper" "internationalism of Putney" (ll. 95f.).

OPINION

7. Is it possible, necessary or even desirable for a country to face four ways like Britain does?

PROJECT

8. Examine the problems and challenges Britain faces a) within Britain b) with Europe c) with the United States and d) with the rest of the world.

14 Britain and Europe get closer together*

Norman Davies

In this extract the historian Norman Davies outlines those social, economic and political forces that have, over the last hundred years, brought the United Kingdom and continental Europe ever closer together. – Norman Davies, *The Isles: A History* (London: Macmillan, 1999), pp. 1010–1012.

In the course of the twentieth century the Isles [the British Isles, ed.] were pulled by stages into a position of ever increasing intimacy with the European mainland. In part, the shift could be explained through far-reaching changes in the patterns of communication and trade. In part, and especially in the second half of the century, it could be attributed to the effects of globalization and the ever-diminishing significance of the old sovereign states. But it must also be seen as the cumulative consequence of three key political decisions – in 1914, in 1939 and in 1972. The end result was not in doubt. In the 1890s the United Kingdom of Great Britain and Ireland was still holding on to its traditional 'semi-detached' stance with regard to the Continent. In the 1990s, both the United Kingdom and the Republic of Ireland were permanently and institutionally engaged in the European Union.

The revolution in communications was there for all to see. If mid-Victorian travellers were thrilled to get from London to Paris in a single day, their mid-century counterparts a hundred years later were accustomed to make the journey in less than an hour. Regular air services round Europe began in the 1920s. Initially, they were very uncomfortable, very expensive, and very exclusive. But from the 1960s commercial jets put air travel within almost everyone's reach. Package holidays boomed. For the first time in history, ordinary British working-class families could take their holidays in Greece, in Italy, or in Spain. On the Mediterranean beaches, and in the *tavernas*, they met millions of other Europeans enjoying themselves in exactly the same way. Their ability to mingle, especially linguistically, was not perfect. But they came back home with the fruits of a learning experience such as no previous generation had been given. They developed a taste for wine; they took a liking to *moussaka*, *pizza*, and *paella*; and they learned the inestimable lesson that the British way of doing things was not necessarily the best. Indeed, if one needed to bag a deckchair and a beach umbrella, the German habit of rising at six o'clock proved rather more effective than the British habit of rising at eight or nine. By the 1990s, a family trip to Corfu or to the Costa del Sol was just as routine as their grandparents' outing to Blackpool or Brighton. What is more, the tavernas of Brighton were matched by the chip shops on Corfu.

Every other form of communication developed at the same dizzy pace. Roll-on, roll-off car ferries replaced cargo ships that had winched tourists' vehicles onto the open deck with a crane. Hovercraft overtook the ferries. Motorways on either side of the Channel put Brussels as close to London as Manchester had been. High-speed rail links – speedier in some countries than others – whisked travellers to and fro with famous despatch. Money-changing, which was once done clumsily with travellers' cheques and suspicious bank clerks, could now be effected instantly at Continental ATMs that accepted British cards. Satellite TV brought Continental programmes into British living rooms. The ultimate step was taken in 1994, when the Channel

"If it weren't for Nelson, we'd all be speaking French... drinking wine... working a 38-hour week, taking August off... bloody Nelson"

Tunnel was opened. One could travel from Folkestone to Boulogne by land. Great Britain had ceased to be an island for the first time in seven thousand years.

Globalization drove similar changes in the organisational sphere. All manner of operations once conducted by local or national organisations were now taken over by international bodies that bestrode frontiers and oceans. The phenomenon was by no means limited to Europe. Indeed, its motive force could often be traced to the USA. But it was particularly relevant to a European continent that had hitherto been fragmented by dozens of sovereign states. Indeed, it promised to give Europe the same economic, transportational and commercial benefits that a huge country like the USA enjoyed. Early steps were taken by international organizations in the postal and transportation spheres. Large multinational firms, like Royal Dutch Shell (1907), were already in existence before the First World War. By the end of the century, there was no important activity in Europe that was not run, regulated, or coordinated by some sort of transnational authority. Britain was locked into the lives of its neighbours as never before.

Changing British trade patterns revealed a growing concentration on export and import with Europe. The trend was in progress several decades before the demise of the British Empire; but it provided a ready-made alternative when 'imperial preference' came to an end in the 1960s. Thanks to the contiguity of the Continent, it developed further and faster than Britain's second line of commercial expansion with the USA. The Confederation of British Industry (CBI) inevitably grew into a fundamental supporter of 'pro-European' sentiment.

Vocabulary

7 to be attributed to (v.): to be believed to be caused by – **13 semi-detached** (adj.): here: not completely believing in s.th. – **13 stance** (n.): opinion – **36 to mingle** (v.): to mix with and meet other people – **43 inestimable** (adj.): (fml.) very great, too much to be calculated – **46 to bag** (v.): (infml.) to reserve s.th. that a lot of people want – **53 to be matched by** (v.): here: to have s.th. similar or have a similar function – **56 dizzy** (adj.): here: very fast – **56 roll-on roll-off** (adj.): a roll-on roll-off ship is one that vehicles can drive straight on and off – **57 to winch** (v.): to lift s.th. with a machine using a rope or chain – **62 to whisk** (v.): here: to transport s.o. quickly – **63 despatch** (n.): here: speed – **75 to bestride** (v. past tense bestrode): here: to cross easily – **95 demise** (n.): /dɪˈmaɪz/ (fml.) the end of s.th. that used to exist – **97 contiguity** (n.): the state of being next to s.th. – **102 sentiment** (n.): (fml.) opinion or feeling you have about s.th.

Explanations

10 1914: the decision by the British government to declare war on Germany at the beginning of the First World War because of the German invasion of Belgium – **10 1939:** the decision by the British government to declare war on Germany because of the German invasion of Poland. This started the Second World War. – **11 1972:** the decision by the British government to apply to join the European Community, now the European Union; the law to make Britain a member was signed in 1972 and Britain officially became a member on 1 January 1973. – **18 mid-Victorian** (adj.): in the middle of the reign of Queen Victoria (1837-1901) – **66 ATM:** automated teller machine; a machine outside a bank that you use to get money from your account; also called a cash dispenser, cash machine or cash point – **85 Royal Dutch Shell:** an Anglo-Dutch oil company, one of the first multinational companies – **96 imperial preference:** a system which gave trading advantages to countries which were members of the British Empire and Commonwealth – **100 Confederation of British Industry:** an employers' organisation which tries to influence the government and promote the interests of its members

AWARENESS

1 What are some of the ways in which Britain and the rest of Europe have been getting closer together since the beginning of the twentieth century? Bear in mind that the traffic between them is two-way, i.e. from Britain to Europe and from Europe to Britain. Write your ideas down under the following headings: food and drink; music, film, radio and television; clothing; transport and leisure; business, trade and commerce; politics; language.

COMPREHENSION

2 Explain what is meant by "old sovereign states" (l. 8).
3 What does Norman Davies mean when he writes that the *tavernas* of Brighton "were matched by the chip shops on Corfu" (ll. 53f.)?
4 Which operations and organisations is Norman Davis referring to when he writes that "All manner of operations once conducted by local or national organisations were now taken over by international bodies ..." (ll. 73ff.)?

Britain in Europe

5 In what ways, according to Norman Davies, is Europe becoming similar to the United States?
6 What has been the great transformation in Britain's pattern of trade in the last fifty or sixty years?

ANALYSIS

7 What have been the effects on Britain of closer links with continental Europe?
8 How, according to Norman Davies, has Britain affected continental Europe over the past one hundred years?
9 In what ways were the "three key political decisions – in 1914, 1939 and in 1972" (ll. 10f.) so decisive for Britain and for Europe?

OPINION

10 The author states that the motive force for globalisation can be traced to the United States. What do you think these American influences on globalisation might be?
11 Speculate on what alternative scenarios might have arisen if Britain had not taken part in the First and Second World Wars or had not joined the European Union.

PROJECT

12 Examine the role of one aspect of either communication (travel, package holidays, the media, transport) and globalisation (multinational companies, international organisations, trade) in bringing Britain and Europe closer together.

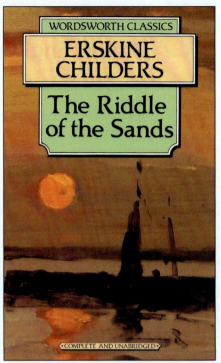

Erskine Childers' spy novel The Riddle of the Sands *is a famous example of alternative history writing*

Alternative history – fiction and non-fiction

The literary genre alternative (or alternate) history is related to and borders on other genres such as fantasy and science fiction but differs from them in that its works are based on real historical events. Writers in alternative history ask themselves the question "What if?": what if a particular historical event had for a number of more or less plausible reasons taken a different turn?

The earliest example of alternative history is probably Book IX, sections 17–19, of Livy's *History of Rome from its Foundation* in which he contemplates the possibility of Alexander the Great expanding his father's empire westward instead of eastward by attacking Rome instead of Persia in the 4th century BC. One of the first alternative novels in English was *The Battle of Dorking*, written by George Chesney in 1871. This was the first of a number of novels inspired by the perceived threat of Imperial Germany to Britain and the British Empire and was followed by Erskine Childers' *The Riddle of the Sands* (1903), *The Invasion of 1910*, by William le Queux (1906), and H. H. Monro's (Saki) *When William Came* (1914). Other notable alternative history novels are Philip K. Dick's *The Man in the High Castle* (1962), in which Nazi Germany and Imperial Japan win the Second World War, Robert Harris's *Fatherland*, in which Nazi Germany wins the Second World War, and Philip Roth's *The Plot against America*, in which a United States governed by a fascist regime under President Charles Lindbergh does not enter the Second World War but maintains peaceful relations with Nazi Germany. The most prolific writer of the genre is Harry Turtledove, in one of whose novels, *Ruled Britannia*, the Spanish Armada defeats the English fleet, enabling Spain to successfully invade England.

While some academic historians completely reject speculative history and the asking of the "What if?" question, others, mainly military historians[1], find it a fruitful area of study. The question "What if?" is already implied in the title of Richard Overy's *Why the Allies Won* and in the heading of the first chapter, "Unpredictable Victory: Explaining World War II". Overy himself does indeed go on to state: To ask why the Allies won is to presuppose that they might have lost or, for understandable reasons, that they would have accepted an outcome short of total victory.[2]

1) Robert Cowley (ed.), *What If? Military Historians Imagine What Might Have Been*, London: Pan, 2001
2) Richard Overy, *Why the Allies Won, London:* Pimlico, 1996, p. 1

15 Malcolm Bradbury

Broken English*

The English language is both a link and a barrier in the relationship between Britain and the rest of Europe. It is a link because as a lingua franca it enables the people of Europe to communicate with each other; it is a barrier because of the many misunderstandings a poor command of English can lead to. – Malcolm Bradbury, *Rates of Exchange* (London: Secker and Warburg, 1983), pp. 61 ff.

Plot Outline

In his novel *Rates of Exchange*, set in 1980s Communist-ruled central Europe, Malcolm Bradbury satirises the strange version of English that native speakers of English meet in their travels in Europe: a language that bears some relationship to English but is full of phonological, lexical and syntactic idiosyncrasies. He also highlights the awkward social interaction, veering between over-familiarity and rudeness, that can occur between people from different cultures. In this extract the linguistics lecturer Dr Petworth arrives in the fictional country of Slaka, in order to take part in an academic conference. He fails to meet the representative from the Ministry of Culture sent to welcome him and so has to negotiate his way through immigration and customs on his own. Then he loses his luggage. Desperately he tries to get help from a young woman at the state travel agency Cosmoplot.

Just behind the Cosmoplot stall, the armed man still stands there, talking to the girl in the grey coat. 'Please,' says Petworth to him, 'Do you speak English? Someone has stolen my luggage.' 'Va?' says the armed man, turning, his nose hard and fierce, his gun swinging on its short strap. 'Va?' 'My luggage,' cries Petworth, 'Stolen!' 'Please,' says the girl in grey, 'He does not understand you. But I know how to interpret. Describe please these luggages to me, and I will explain you.' 'Thank you,' says Petworth, turning gratefully to the girl, who has a white tense face, a mohair hat on her head, a shoulderbag over her shoulder; and in her hands and at her feet a blue suitcase, a bulging briefcase, a heavy overcoat, and a plastic bag which says 'Say Hello to the Good Buys at Heathrow.' 'What consists your luggages?' says the girl, patiently, 'Please explain it. He is a policeman and likes to help.' 'That's my luggage, there,' says Petworth, 'You've got it.' 'These?' says the girl, staring at him, 'No, these are not your luggages.' 'I left them over there, by that pillar,' says Petworth. 'But they are not your luggages,' says the girl, firmly, 'They are the luggages of another. They belong to Professor Petworth.' 'Exactly,' says Petworth, 'Me.' 'He comes from England to make some lectures,' says the girl. 'Yes,' says Petworth, 'I'm Petworth.' 'Oh, do you like to think so?' says the girl, looking at him and laughing, 'Well, I am sorry, you are not.' 'I'm not?' asks Petworth. 'No, really you are not,' says the girl, 'I have his photograph, sent from Britain. Do you think you are that man?' Petworth looks at the photograph; it shows a large round balding face, of late middle age, wearing heavy glasses, and underneath it the legend Dr W. Petworth. 'Well, no,' Petworth admits, 'That's someone else.' 'I have looked three hour for this man,' says the girl, 'Now I find his luggage. But it is not you. You do not even look like a professor.' 'I'm not, yet,' says Petworth, 'But I am Petworth.' 'You are not,' says the girl, 'Please go away.'

'Wait, I think I know who that is,' says Petworth, pointing at the photograph, 'That's another Petworth, who teaches at the University of Watermouth, I get his mail sometimes. He's not very well known.' 'And you, who are you?' asks the girl; the armed man steps nearer. 'Well, I'm an even less well-known Petworth than he is,' Petworth admits, 'But I'm the one they sent.' The armed man pokes Petworth with his fingers: 'Dikumenti,' he says. It is a happy intervention, for out comes the grey letter from the Min'stratii Kulturi Komitet'iii, which the girl seizes. 'Oh, oh, yes, you are the one, really!' she cries, 'Oh, Petwurt, you have

confused me, you do not look like yourself. And there I waited for two hour at INVAT, to bring you past the custom, but I looked for that man with the big head. Well, no matter, it is just a small confusion, quickly solved.' 'Then you're from the Ministratii Kulturi Komitet'iii?' asks Petworth. 'Oh, Petwurt,' the girl says admiringly, looking at him with her white, saddened face, 'You are in Slaka just three hour and already you speak our language. Actually we say it so: Min'stratii. Do you see the difference? You intrude a redundant "i." But that is natural error for an English. Yes, I am from there, your guide for this tour. My name is Marisja Lubijova, Oh dear, that is hard for you. Do you think you can say it?' 'Yes,' says Petworth, 'Marisja Lubijova.' 'Very good,' says the girl, 'But I think it is too long for you. You call me Mari, like all my good friends. And in Slaka it is your first time? I don't think so, you speak our language so well.' 'Yes, my first time,' says Petworth. 'Then I welcome you to my country,' says Lubijova, 'Do we do it the English way? How do you do, shake the hand, I wish you very nice visit?' 'What's the Slaka way?' asks Petworth, 'In customs they gave me a comradely hug.'

Marisja Lubijova stares at him: 'Oh, I see, Petwurt,' she says, 'You are only just come but already you want everything. Well, of course, the Min'stratii will not be outdone.' 'I just meant ...' Petworth begins, but the words choke; for two arms come firmly round his neck; he is tugged, forward, downward, into Lubijova's grey coat. This time it is nicer: no male sweat, but the scent of healthy soap; no belt of hard leather, but a delightful mammary cushion; no prodding male groin, but a better mesh of bodily economy, a fairer rate of exchange. 'Camerad'aki,' Lubijova cries, thrusting him back, 'So welcome in Slaka! Oh, dear, Petwurt, your face goes quite red. Perhaps you are shy, like all English.' 'It seemed the right colour for the country,' says Petworth. 'I think you like our customs,' says Lubijova, 'That means you will make good visit. Now, I just tell this policeman all problems are solved. Please take some of your luggages, and we go somewhere. Do you like a nice hotel of the old kind, I hope so?' 'Yes,' says Petworth, sensing he is back on the old course of things, 'I do.' They begin to go, Petworth carrying his recovered luggage, walking with his recovered guide, towards the evening light, the doors marked OTVAT. 'Oh, dear, you must think I am bad guide,' says Lubijova, 'Did you think no one comes for you? I think you did, but you shouldn't. Of course someone finds you, you are important visitor. Everywhere people are waiting to see you, and expecting remarkable talks. Often there are confusions in these places, but no matter. Now we find a very nice taxi. Oh, I please you are here.'

Vocabulary

Intro: lingua franca (n.): a language used between people whose main languages are different – **Plot Outline: idiosyncrasy:** an unusual or unexpected feature that s.th. has – **Plot Outline: to veer** (v.): to change direction – **11 tense** (adj.): not relaxed – **13 briefcase** (n.): a flat case used especially by business people for carrying papers or documents – **31 balding** (adj.): losing one's hair – **60 to intrude** (v.): to put (the transitive use of this verb is very unusual and the verb insert would be expected here) – **60 redundant** (adj.): not necessary or needed – **73 hug** (n.): the action of putting your arms around s.o. and holding them tightly – **77 to outdo** (v.): to be better or more successful than s.o. else at doing s.th. – **78 to choke** (v.): here: to be unable to be pronounced – **79 to tug** (v.): to pull – **82 mammary** (adj.): connected with the breasts – **82 prodding** (adj.): pushing quickly – **82 groin** (n.): the place where the tops of your legs meet the front of your body – **83 mesh** (n.): here: joining together, touching – **83f. rate of exchange** (n.): the value of the money of one country compared to the money of another; also exchange rate

Explanations

15 Heathrow: one of the four main international airports serving London; situated 25 km west of London – **41 University of Watermouth:** fictional English university

A very confusing warning

BURNABLE RUBBISH

MILK or JUICE (PAPER) FRUIT MEAT PAPER PASSPORT

Please threw a way noodle and soup in kitchen's trashcan.

Sign in a takeaway restaurant

AWARENESS
1. Describe what was different about any foreign European country you have visited. Consider the way people talked and interacted, their clothing, manners and gestures, the smells and sounds you were aware of, and the style of the buildings.

COMPREHENSION
2. Explain the advertising slogan on the plastic bag: Say Hello to the Good Buys at Heathrow (l. 14f.).
3. What has happened to Petworth's luggage?
4. How does Petworth convince Marisja Lubijova that he is the right Petworth?
5. Describe the two occasions on which Petworth was greeted on his arrival in Slaka.
6. Why does Petworth blush when embraced by Marisja?

ANALYSIS
7. Translate all of Marisja's utterances into correct English.
8. What mistakes do Dr Petworth and Marisja Lubijova make in their interaction with each other?
9. Analyse the humour of this excerpt.

OPINION
10. Write a short article for foreigners coming to Germany on behaviour they should be aware of when they meet people. Carefully define the social situation you are referring to. You may wish to include some of the following points: a) forms of address (names, use of personal pronouns *Du* and *Sie*), b) ways of greeting (kissing, hugging, embracing, hand-shaking, gestures), c) leave-taking, d) eating habits, e) loudness or quietness of voice, f) sniffing, coughing, sneezing, nose-blowing, g) seating arrangements in meetings, at restaurants, cafés, in homes, h) gifts for hosts, i) making arrangements for private and business visits, j) courtesy to women, k) ways of standing and sitting, l) ways of indicating agreement and disagreement, m) ways of asking people to do something n) small talk, taboo topics, o) accepting and giving compliments. Compare your article with that of other students and discuss what you agree and disagree on.
11. Discuss the examples of problems English speakers have with the use of familiar and polite pronouns in German (Info Box, p. 51). What help can you give to speakers of English on their use?

PROJECT
12. Select a short – three to five minute – video sequence from television or film illustrating social interaction in Britain. This could be an introduction, meeting or leave-taking, a business meeting, a party, a family meal, or a meeting between friends at a pub or café. Analyse the ways in which the interaction in these sequences differs from interaction in similar situations in Germany.
13. Collect a series of four or five photographs from British newspapers and magazines. In groups study each photograph carefully and make a list of those features that you think are different from those in Germany. These might be hair styles, clothing, body language, facial expressions, architectural styles, urban and rural features.

Britain in Europe

"You can say you to me"

For speakers of English the use of second person personal pronouns and names is one the most difficult problems they face in communicating with speakers of European languages. Apart from religious usage and some English dialects, in which *thou* and *thee* still occur, speakers of English use only one pronoun to address others: you. All other European languages make use of two or three pronouns, usually termed familiar (or T form from Latin *tu*) and polite (or V form from Latin *vos*) for addressing others according to the status or familiarity of the addressee.

In English the function of these pronouns has largely been replaced by the use of names, thus Mr John Smith could be addressed by any of the following: Mr Smith, Mr John Smith, Smith, John, or Johnnie. Standard procedure is that in most situations in Britain – meeting new neighbours, new friends and acquaintances and at the workplace – people will immediately use first names. This practice cannot be transferred to continental Europe and certainly not to Germany.

The editor of this book has experienced some of these problems personally. At a dinner party in Germany he was invited to, three different forms of address were in use: use of first name and *Sie* between the host and himself; the use of *Sie* and *Herr* xxx and *Frau* xxx between the editor and the other guests; and the use *Du* and first name between the host and the other guests. The editor's wife still finds it difficult to address neighbours she has known for over twenty years and has met at numerous coffee and cake afternoons using *Sie* and *Frau* xxx. Attempts to overcome this apparent barrier by ignoring it and using first names can meet with disaster as a young English teacher found at an English-language training course for a German company. The German course participants simply refused to address each other using first names in the English lessons and the "friendly" atmosphere that the English teacher had hoped to create was reduced to frosty embarrassment.

16

Jonathan Lynn and Antony Jay

Party Games – Using Europe in British Politics*

The present prime minister and party leader has decided to resign. There are two main contenders: the chancellor of the exchequer, Eric Jeffries, and the foreign secretary, Duncan Short. Both of them have strong support within the party. Jim Hacker, the head of the Department of Administrative Affairs, has been persuaded to consider running as a compromise candidate. As he is relatively unknown he decides to raise his profile by defending British interests in the European Union. – Transcribed from: Jonathan Lynn, Antony Jay, *The Complete Yes Prime Minister. Series One* (BBC Video BBC V 4790, 1989).

1 Jim Hacker: By the end of the year we'll be waving goodbye to the good old British sausage and will be forced to accept some foreign muck like salami or
5 bratwurst or something in its place.
  Bernard Woolley: But they can't stop us eating the British sausage, can they?
  Jim Hacker: They can stop us calling it the sausage, though. Apparently it's got to be called the emulsified high fat offal tube.
10
  Bernard Woolley: And you swallowed it?
  Jim Hacker: It's my job to implement EEC regulations. It could finish my career.
  Bernard Woolley: What have they got against our 15 sausage?
  Jim Hacker: Oh dear, don't you ever read the papers you give me? Apparently there's not enough meat in it. The average British sausage consists of 20 32.5% fat, 6.5% rind, 20% water, 10% rusk, 5% seasoning, preservatives and colouring, and only 26% meat, which is mostly gristle, head meat, other off cuts and mechani- 25 cally recovered meat steamed off the carcass ... I don't feel particularly well. I had one for breakfast.

Sir Humphrey Appleby, Jim Hacker, Bernard Woolley

Bernard Woolley: Perhaps the EEC commissioner is right about abolishing it.

In order to try to sort out the problem of the British sausage, Sir Humphrey Appleby arranges a meeting between Maurice, the European Union commissioner responsible for food who happens to be in London at that time, and Jim Hacker.

Sir Humphrey: Maurice! How very nice to see you.
Maurice: Humphrey! Jim! To what do I owe this pleasure?
Jim Hacker: I er ...
Sir Humphrey: Maurice asked me to arrange this little meeting to see if you could ... erm ... help ... erm ... us with a problem.
Jim Hacker: A problem ...
Maurice: Of course.
Sir Humphrey: Now the problem is that the EEC is becoming very unpopular over here. Isn't that so, minister?
Jim Hacker: Very unpopular.
Maurice: And you want me to restore its image?
Jim Hacker: Yes.
Sir Humphrey: No.
Jim Hacker: No.
Sir Humphrey: And the problem is that the minister feels there would be more votes ... he would be better expressing the views of the British people by joining the attack on the EEC rather than leaping to its defence.
Maurice: But ... but your government is committed to support us.
Jim Hacker: Er ...
Sir Humphrey: The minister's point – as I understand it – is that the government's commitment is to the concept and the treaty ...
Jim Hacker: Treaty ...
Sir Humphrey: It's not committed to the institutions, nor to the practices nor to the individual policies. The minister was giving me an example the other day, weren't you minister?
Jim Hacker: [Nods in agreement]
Sir Humphrey: About food production?
Jim Hacker: Oh yes. I've discovered that one of your officials spends all his time paying farmers to produce masses of surplus food while somebody in the next office pays people to destroy the surpluses.
Maurice: That's not true!
Jim Hacker: [Look of surprise] No?
Maurice: He's not in the next office! He's not even on the same floor!
Sir Humphrey: And the minister has hundreds of similar examples, haven't you?
Jim Hacker: Hundreds.
Sir Humphrey: And the nub of the problem is that the minister thinks that some members of the Cabinet ought to start telling the British people about them.
Maurice: That would be intolerable! Not even the Italians would stoop that low.
Jim Hacker: The Italians haven't been asked to redesignate salami as emulsified high-fat offal tubing.
Maurice: Aah! And what are you proposing? After all we are committed to harmonisation. We cannot call it the sausage. What do you suggest?
Sir Humphrey: Well, politics is about presentation. Why don't we call it the British sausage?
Maurice: British sausage? Sausisse anglaise? Britischer [sic] Wurst? Yes, I think we could recommend that to the Commission.
Sir Humphrey: Splendid. The minister's always said that the EEC is a splendid institution, haven't you, minister?
Jim Hacker: Splendid! [Jim Hacker kisses Maurice on the cheek]

Jim Hacker is preparing to meet the newspaper reporters and correspondents of the press lobby at the Department of Administrative Affairs.

Bernard Woolley: The European correspondents are all here now, minister.
Jim Hacker: Good, let them in.
Bernard Woolley: [On the intercom] Will you send them in. Presumably this is to tell them about the Eurosausage problem.
Jim Hacker: That's right, Bernard.
Bernard Woolley: And that you've solved it.
Jim Hacker: Well, no, Bernard. Solved problems aren't news stories. To the press bad news is good news. I'm not going to give them a non-story today. I'm going to give them a disaster today and a triumph tomorrow.
Bernard Woolley: I see ...

Newspaper reporters and correspondents enter Jim Hacker's room.

Jim Hacker: Good morning gentlemen. Come in. Do sit down. So good of you to come. Now look, all of this is on a lobby basis, non-attributable. But we've got some trouble coming up with Brussels. As I suppose somebody's going to tell you about it anyway some time, I'd better tell you about it now myself. The trouble is that Brussels is about to make the British sausage illegal under EEC regulations.
Bernard Woolley: [whispers] They're not making the sausage illegal, just the name.
Jim Hacker: Thank you Bernard. I'll be dealing with that later.
Journalist A: What do you mean, illegal?
Jim Hacker: Well, effectively illegal. The pork sausage will have to contain 75% lean pork. The same for the beef sausage.
Journalist B: 75% pork too?
Jim Hacker: 75% lean beef. Which of course would put it in the luxury food bracket.
Journalist C: When is this being promulgated?
Jim Hacker: Next month probably. They'll deny it of course. Probably they'll say they're just discussing changing its name or something.
Journalist D: What is the government going to do about it?
Jim Hacker: I just don't know. It's a big problem. I won't pretend we've got an answer. All right. Well, I must rush. That's all I've got for now. Is that all? Any more questions?
Journalist E: When can we use this?
Jim Hacker: Tomorrow as far as I'm concerned. Right. Bernard'll give you a drink in the Press Office. Thank you so much for coming.
Bernard Woolley: Minister, you do realise the press will be publishing something that isn't true?
Jim Hacker: Really? How frightful.

Jim Hacker and Bernard Woolley are in their car driving to where Jim Hacker is going to make a speech, apparently on fire and safety regulations in government buildings. They are listening to the news on BBC radio.

Newsreader: Today's big story about the proposed European ban on the British sausage has caused a major political storm. Westminster sources say the sausage could be another banana skin. It adds to the government's problems with the succession. Senior people in the party are increasingly troubled that the two senior candidates represent the extreme wings of the party. Pressure is mounting for them to withdraw in favour of a compromise candidate. None of the other contenders so far seem to have caught the public imagination. Now sport ...
Jim Hacker: Turn it off.
Bernard Woolley: Is that true about the compromise candidate?
Jim Hacker: I believe so.
Bernard Woolley: Where do they get their information from?
Jim Hacker: I can't imagine, Bernard. In any case, I never said "compromise", I said "moderate".
Bernard Woolley: Incidentally, minister, why are BBC Television and ITN covering your speech this evening?
Jim Hacker: I can't imagine, Bernard.
Bernard Woolley: I mean, I know that fire and safety policy in government buildings is awfully important, but ...
Jim Hacker: Someone suggested I was going to raise other issues as well.
Bernard Woolley: Who?
Jim Hacker: I can't imagine.

Jim Hacker's speech

I'm a good European. I believe in Europe. I believe in the European ideal! Never again shall we repeat the bloodshed of two world wars. Europe is here to stay.

But, this does not mean that we have to bow the knee to every directive from every bureaucratic Bonaparte in Brussels. We are a sovereign nation still and proud of it. (applause)

We have made enough concessions to the European Commissar for agriculture. And when I say Commissar, I use the word advisedly. We have swallowed the wine lake, we have swallowed the butter mountain, we have watched our French 'friends' beating up British lorry drivers carrying good British lamb to the French public.

We have bowed and scraped, doffed our caps, tugged our forelocks and turned the other cheek. But I say enough is enough! (prolonged applause)

The Europeans have gone too far. They are now threatening the British sausage. They want to standardize it – by which they mean they'll force the British people to eat salami and bratwurst and other garlic-ridden greasy foods that are TOTALLY ALIEN to the British way of life. (cries of "hear hear!", "right on", and "you tell 'em Jim!")

Do you want to eat salami for breakfast with your egg and bacon? I don't. And I won't! (massive applause)

GO TO WORK ON A SAUSAGE!

They've turned our pints into litres and our yards into metres. We gave up the tanner and the threepenny bit, the two bob and half crown. But they cannot and will not destroy the British sausage! (applause and cheers)

Not while I'm here. (tumultuous applause)

In the words of Martin Luther: 'Here I stand. I can do no other.'

Jim Hacker's use of anti-European feelings in Britain was successful. His rivals for the leadership of his party withdrew and Jim Hacker gained the leadership of his party unopposed.

Info

The main characters in this episode of *Yes, Prime Minister*

Jim Hacker: Secretary of State for Administrative Affairs, head of the Department of Administrative Affairs
Maurice: (surname not mentioned) European Union (at that time European Economic Community) Commissioner
Bernard Woolley: Principal Private Secretary, a civil servant in the Department of Administrative Affairs
Sir Humphrey Appleby: Permanent Secretary, the senior civil servant in the Department of Administrative Affairs

Vocabulary

Intro: contender (n.): s.o. who is in competition with other people – **4 muck** (n.): s.th. that is unpleasant or of bad quality – **10 emulsified** (adj.): combined with other substances to become a smooth mixture – **10 offal** (n.): the inside parts of an animal – **12 to swallow** (v.): (word play) to make food or drink go down your throat and towards your stomach; to believe s.th. that is not actually true – **21 rind** (n.): /raɪnd/ here: the thick outer skin of some kinds of meat – **22 rusk** (n.): here: hard dry bread – **22 seasoning** (n.): salt, pepper, spices that give food a more interesting flavour – **22 preservative** (n): a chemical substance that is used to prevent food from going bad – **24 gristle** (n.): the part of meat that is not soft enough to eat – **25 off cuts** (n.): here: pieces of meat that are left over after the main pieces have been cut and removed – **63 to be committed to s.th.** (v.): to be willing to work very hard at s.th. – **67 commitment** (n.): being ready to work very hard for s.th. or s.o. – **83 surplus** (adj.): more than what is needed – **94 nub** (n.): the main point – **100 to stoop low** (v.): to do s.th. bad or morally wrong – **101 to redesignate** (v.): to give s.th. a new name – **126 intercom** (n.): a communication system by which people in different parts of a building, aircraft, etc. can speak to each other – **127 presumably** (adj.): used to say that you think s.th. is probably true – **144 non-attributable** (adj.): used when journalists agree not to say who made a statement or comment – **160 lean** (adj.): lean meat does not have much fat on it – **165 bracket** (n.): here: group of products – **166 to promulgate** (v.): (fml.) to make a new law come into effect – **191 proposed** (adj.): suggested as a plan or course of action – **192 ban** (n.): an official order that prevents s.th. being sold, done, etc. – **197 succession** (n.): the act of taking over an official position, here: of prime minister – **216 incidentally** (adv.): here: used to introduce a new topic that you have just thought of – **224 to raise an issue** (v.): to introduce a topic that you

Britain in Europe

want to be considered – **230 bloodshed** (n.): the killing of people, usually in war – **235 concession** (n.): s.th. that you allow s.o. to have or to do in order to end an argument – **237 advisedly** (adv.): /ədˈvaɪzɪdli/ after careful thought – **241 to bow and scrape** (v.): to show too much respect to s.o. – **241 to doff one's cap** (v.): (old-fash.) to take off the hat you are wearing as a sign of respect – **241f. to tug one's forelock** (v.): to show too much respect for s.o. in authority

Explanations

Intro: chancellor of the exchequer: the minister in the British government who is responsible for financial matters – **Intro: foreign secretary:** the minister in the British government who is responsible for relations with other countries – **13 EEC:** European Economic Community; the first name for what was then named the European Community and is now called the European Union. – **25f. mechanically recovered meat:** meat that is taken off bones by machines and used to make sausages and hamburgers – **96 Cabinet:** the politicians with important positions in the government who meet to make decisions – **121 press lobby:** a group of journalists and correspondents with privileged access to government information as long as they did not say who gave them the information – **181 Press Office:** this British government office deals with the prime minister's relations with the media. – **190 BBC:** British Broadcasting Corporation; the British radio and television company that is paid for by viewers' and listeners' licence money and not by advertisers. – **195 banana skin:** (humorous) here: used to refer to s.th. that causes problems or difficulties – **232 directive:** an official order or instruction – **236 Commissar:** an official of the Communist Party of the former Soviet Union and of Communist China, responsible for political education and organisation – **Info Box: secretary of state:** chief minister of a department or ministry of the British government – **Department** (n.): usual word for ministry in the British government – **Department of Administrative Affairs:** a fictitious ministry that only occurs in the TV series *Yes Minister* and *Yes Prime Minister* – **Commissioner:** a member of the Commission of the European Union which is headed by the President; responsible for administering and implementing the policies and decisions of the members of the EU – **Principal Private Secretary:** a senior member of the civil service, the British government bureaucracy – **civil servant:** a member of the civil service, the British government bureaucracy

Awareness
1 Why do you think so many British people are sceptical about Britain's membership of the European Union?

Comprehension
2 Why can't the British continue to call a sausage a sausage?
3 Is it true that there is an official in the Commission of the EU who spends his time paying people to destroy food surpluses?
4 How does Maurice solve the problem of the British sausage?
5 Does the EU want to forbid the British from producing the British sausage?
6 Why doesn't Jim Hacker want to tell the journalists that he has solved the problem of the British sausage?
7 Who told the BBC that a compromise candidate for the leadership of the party might be putting himself forward?
8 Why are BBC TV and ITN covering Jim Hacker's speech?

Analysis
9 Analyse the conversation between Sir Humphrey Appleby, Maurice and Jim Hacker. Look at the roles of each of them, the way their language expresses the relationship between them, their aims in the conversation and their rhetorical strategies for achieving those aims.
10 In the conversation between Sir Humphrey Appleby, Maurice and Jim Hacker, Jim Hacker is made to seem rather stupid. Explain what characteristics he has that enable him to achieve such high office in the British government.
11 What is the point of the meeting between Jim Hacker and the journalists?
Explain Jim Hacker's strategy at the meeting.
12 Analyse Jim Hacker's speech on "fire and safety regulations in government buildings".
Consider what he says, how he says it and why he says it.
Discuss the function of the imagery used, the examples cited, rhetorical questions, use of voice, parallelisms and phrases in groups of three.

Opinion
13 What is your opinion of the cynicism regarding the European Union displayed by Jim Hacker and Sir Humphrey Appleby?
14 Write a letter to Jim Hacker in response to his speech.

Project
15 Write a report on the advantages and disadvantages for Germany of membership of the European Union.

17 Steve Thoburn – the Metric Martyr*

T. R. Reid

Among the many EU regulations there is one that requires that all fresh produce sold in the EU be priced and weighed in metric measures. Traditionally, all goods in Britain have been manufactured and marketed in non-metric sizes and quantities: pounds and ounces for weights, pints, quarts and gallons for liquids, inches, feet, yards, and miles for distances. The introduction of metric units for weights meant customers and shopkeepers had to get accustomed to this system when shopping for their daily needs. Some were not very happy about this and a few, like Steve Thoburn (1964–2004), refused to conform. – T. R. Reid, *The United States of Europe* (London: Penguin Books, 2004), pp. 58 ff.

Steve Thoburn

And then there is EU Directive 80-181-EEC, the pan-European regulation that made greengrocer Steve Thoburn a national hero – a reluctant one, but a hero nonetheless – in Great Britain.

In the rusty shipbuilding town of Sunderland, England – the ancestral home of George Washington – Steve did a bustling trade hour after hour at the tiny market stall he ran, "Thoburn's Fruit and Veg." The place is a veritable EU of greenery: Steve sold Dutch leeks, Spanish peppers, French apples, British spinach, and Greek olives, all neatly stacked and marked with country of origin and price per pound in Steve's firm hand. "I label everything," Steve explained. "I want me customers to know what they're buying."

An intense but likeable thirty-something with curly hair and a gold ring in his right ear, Steve was caught red-handed weighing and selling bananas by the pound. He was charging 34 pence per pound. This was a bargain price, by English standards, but the sale was a blatant violation of EU Directive 80-181-EEC, a regulation requiring that fresh produce sold in any EU country must be priced and weighed in metric measures – that is litres and kilograms. Under a statute incorporating EU trade regulations into British law, Steve was charged with violating the Weights and Measures Act. Prosecutors said this was simply a matter of enforcing the law; Steve, though, saw an official conspiracy against small business. "They're after me because all I have is this little market," he said. "Anybody in this town can still go to a McDonald's and buy a Quarter-Pounder. Why doesn't that have to be a 113-Grammer?" (In fact, McDonald's outlets throughout Europe are required to list the metric proportions of all their food and drink items.)

Anyway, Steve went on, the women of Sunderland had always bought bananas by the pound, and they wanted to continue. Steve Thoburn was determined "to give me customers what they want." Accordingly, he stubbornly refused to replace his pound-and-ounce scale with a metric version, even when the town prosecutor indicated that Thoburn's Fruit and Veg could face fines equal to £9,000 if convicted on the two pending counts.

Britain's national newspapers had a field day with the story – they dubbed Thoburn the "Metric Martyr" – and Eurosceptics across the nation adopted him as the symbol of their anti-Brussels campaign. On a chilly January day, Steve went on trial in Sunderland Magistrate's Court; the judge declared that the case centred on "the most famous bunch of bananas in British legal history". Inside the courthouse, Steve was represented by a high-powered defence lawyer who had been hired by a national Eurosceptic organization and imported from London to argue the case. Outside, a noisy crowd was waving flags, banners, and bananas. Their poster read: "Metric Martyr on trial here! Hoot to support!"

Some passing motorists did hoot their horns that morning, but many others drove past silently. Even in Sunderland, an insular, self-contained city in the north of England, feelings about Brussels and the European Union were mixed. It was easy, of course, to build up an indignant head of steam against arrogant foreign regulators, daft government rules, and prosecutors determined to turn a pound of bananas into a federal case. On the other hand, there was hesitation in the city about attacking the European Union. At the dawn of the twenty-first century, the EU had become crucial to Sunderland's well-being. The few contracts still being awarded at the ageing, inefficient shipyards along the river Wear were largely funded by EU grants to local fishermen and shipping companies. And the largest single employer in Sunderland these days is a new Nissan plant, located there specifically to give the Japanese auto maker a European presence. By building its cars in an EU nation, Nissan can export to any other EU member country free of tariffs, duties, and regulatory hassles.

Even Steve Thoburn was ambivalent. When I went up to Sunderland to meet the Metric Martyr, Steve complained that he was thoroughly uncomfortable with that title, and the way his case had been turned into political fodder for the anti-EU campaigners. "I don't give a toss about politics," Thoburn said, carefully arranging matching hillocks of red and green peppers on his market shelves. "I've never cast a vote. I have nothing against metrics. If somebody came into me premises and says, 'C'mon, luv, give us a kilo of bananas,' I'd sell it to her. But nobody ever asks for that."

Steve had no particular problem with the European Union, either, or with the Eurocrats, or with Brussels. In fact, the day I dropped by Thoburn's Fruit and Veg, the special offer of the day was none other than brussels sprouts. "Oh, I love brussels sprouts," Steve told me, holding a firm green specimen between thumb and forefinger. "You put this on the roast platter on Sunday, and that's the king of veg."

Despite the efforts of that high-powered London lawyer and his political backers, the Metric Martyr was convicted on two counts in the town court. The Eurosceptics then launched a series of high-profile appeals, promising to go to Britain's highest court, or even to the European Court of Justice, which can overrule the top British judge. All that seemed likely to delay a final decision in the case for years. Steve Thoburn, with his fines on hold while the legal battle went forward, did his best to get back to the business of selling fruit and vegetables. When customers said, "C'mon, luv, give us a pound of bananas," he did exactly that. His message to the European Union was simple: "Leave a bloke alone so he can give his customers what they want."

Vocabulary

Intro: shilling (n.): an old British coin which went out of use in 1971. There were 20 shillings in one pound. - **3 reluctant** (adj.): unwilling - **6 ancestral** (adj.): connected with members of your family who lived a long time ago - **7 bustling** (adj.): very busy - **9 veritable** (adj.): real, true - **10 leek** (n.): a vegetable with a long white stem and long flat green leaves, which tastes like an onion - **10 pepper** (n.): a round-shaped hollow red, green or yellow vegetable - **10 spinach** (n.): /'spɪnɪdʒ/ a vegetable with large dark green leaves - **11 to stack** (v.): to make things into a neat pile - **13 me** (det): dialect for my - **16f. to catch s.o. red-handed** (v.): to catch s.o. at the moment they are doing s.th. wrong - **20 blatant** (adj.): s.th. bad that is blatant is very clear and easy to see - **20 violation** (n.): an action that breaks a law - **25 to charge s.o. with s.th.** (v.): to state officially that s.o. may be guilty of a crime - **26 prosecutor** (n.): the public official who states that s.o. may be guilty of a crime and starts a court case - **28 conspiracy** (n.): a secret plan - **43 pending** (adj.): waiting to be dealt with - **43 count** (n.): one of the crimes s.o. is charged with - **44 to have a field day with s.th.** (v.): to have the chance to do a lot of s.th. you want - **45 to dub** (v.): to give s.o. a name that describes them in some way - **61f. to build up a head of steam** (v.): to become very active after starting s.th. slowly - **63 daft** (adj.): /dɑft/ stupid - **70 grant** (n.): an amount of money given to s.o. esp. by the government - **77 hassle** (n.): s.th. that is annoying because it causes problems - **82 fodder** (n.): s.th. that is useful only for a particular purpose - **83 not to give a toss about s.th.** (v.): - (infml.) to not care about s.th. at all - **84 hillock** (n.): a small hill, pile - **94 brussels sprout** (n.): a small round green vegetable (*Rosenkohl*) - **106 on hold** (adj.): waiting to be dealt with - **110 bloke** (n.): (infml.) man

Explanations

1 EU Directive: an official order or instruction issued by the European Union - **1 pan-European:** for the whole of the European Union - **5 Sunderland:** an industrial town in northeast England, with a population of 280,000 - **6 George Washington:** (1732-99) American general and statesman; first president of the United States 1789-97; Washington helped win the War of Independence by winning a decisive battle at Yorktown (1781); his ancestors came from Washington Village in the county of Tyne and Wear near Sunderland. - **25f. Weights and Measures Act:** the law which determines what units should be used to measure object and liquids - **46 Eurosceptic** (n.): s.o. who is against Britain's membership of the European Union - **47 Brussels:** the capital city of Belgium and symbol of the European Union - **48f. Magistrate's Court:** law courts in England which deal with less serious crimes - **64f. federal case:** here: a serious crime - **73 Nissan plant:** car factory built by the Nissan Motor Company (UK) and the largest in Brtitain; since the plant was opened in 1986 more than 4 million cars have been built there. - **87 luv:** eye dialect for love, pronounced /lʌv/ in the north of England; a common form of address in Britain - **87 us:** commonly used in speech in Britain for me - **91 Eurocrat:** (infml.) a high-ranking official of the European Union; formed from the words European and aristocrat - **103 European Court of Justice:** sits in Luxembourg and was created to settle conflicts between the states, the organs of the European Union and between the states and the organs of the EU. - **108 C'mon:** (infml.) come on

AWARENESS

1 How does Germany's membership of the European Union affect you personally? Do you feel that there are any advantages or disadvantages for you?

COMPREHENSION

2. What did Steve Thoburn think was the real reason he was being prosecuted for selling fruit and vegetables by the pound instead of by grams and kilograms? What evidence did he have for this belief?
3. Why did Steve Thoburn continuing to sell fruit and vegetables by the pound?
4. Why did Steve Thoburn not get full support from the people of Sunderland?
5. Why was Steve Thoburn himself "ambivalent" (l. 78) about his own campaign to sell his fruit and vegetables by the pound?

ANALYSIS

6. State in factual terms the case for a) Steve Thoburn, b) the prosecution and c) the Eurosceptics.

OPINION

7. Imagine you are either a) the prosecution counsel or b) the defence counsel for Steve Thoburn. Write a suitable final plea to be presented to the court.
8. Write a letter to the local Sunderland newspaper in which you give your personal opinion on Steve Thoburn's campaign and his prosecution by the authorities.

PROJECT

9. Using the Internet write a report giving more background information about Steve Thoburn, about the situation in Sunderland and the aid it gets from the EU and about how the Eurosceptics made use of Steve Thoburn's campaign.

18

Henry Porter

What we want from Europe

In this newspaper article a number of writers and journalists were asked what they would most like to import into Britain from Europe. Their answers included shaking hands, Italian women, pharmacies, classlessness, male elegance, the Friesian landscape, the bidet, campsites and the siesta. However only one – Italian women – could be chosen for this anthology. – Henry Porter, The Sunday Telegraph Telegraph Magazine, no date, p. 35.

ITALIAN WOMEN

My first exposure to Italian women came when, as a student in Perugia, I watched the *passaggiata*. This informal promenade, which took place twice a day, at noon and 6 pm, is the sort of shameless display that the British cannot understand, but which the Italians love. If you are a mother with a young baby, a man with a new coat, a young woman with a beautiful body, you show it off at every opportunity. It is pure vanity, but it is also a demonstration of self-respect.

I was fresh from ten years in English boarding schools and utterly unprepared for the parade of Italian womanhood: the teenage girls who linked arms and swayed along the streets giggling at the admiration they drew; the new mothers, serene and slightly fatigued; and the women in their late 30s and 40s who walked and shopped and gossiped, napalming the men with chic and experienced sex appeal.

I looked hard at the young men who lounged alone in the cafés and realised that they were no less affected than me: their nonchalance was a fake. The point was soon grasped. An Italian woman can turn on a look of such powerful suggestion that it all but disables the masculine nervous system. There are many plain women in Italy, but most of them have the ability to flash this

The passaggiata in Milan

look which makes one instantly forget their limited potential as *femmes fatales* and the nightmare that awaits you in 30 or 40 years of a marriage bed.

It took me many more months of living in Italy and watching the *passaggiata* to conclude that the country is entirely feminine. Men are forced to compete on the terms set out by the insuperable beauty and wisdom of their women. This is why masculinity in Italy can be so exaggerated and cruel. The histrionic behaviour of men in politics, sport or even while driving a car, is an act of foot-stamping rebellion against the mother's power. Every man in Italy is, in some way, placed in the position of asking forgiveness from his woman, which means he might as well behave badly.

Twenty years ago, it was not unusual for a couple to be chaperoned. On my first date with a saintly looking girl called Francesca we were accompanied by her aunt, a solid little person who sat behind us for the showing of the film *Zabriskie Point*. Throughout the film she muttered a combination of her rosary and a shopping list: '*Ave Maria ... patate e pollo e pomodori ... santo spirito.*' When a sex scene came on the screen she leant forward to distract Francesca by talking about the local priest. It was like being placed under surveillance by an extreme Catholic organisation.

Once we were outside the cinema she made some enquiries about me. I told her I was an English student. '*Ah inglese! Va bene!*' She kissed her niece goodnight and stumped off laughing: in Italy the English are regarded as having practically no sex drive. [...]

Typical? A young Italian woman

Vocabulary

2 exposure (n.): the chance to experience new ideas, ways of life, etc. – **13 vanity** (n.): too much pride in yourself, so that you are always thinking about yourself and your appearance – **17 boarding school** (n.): school where students live as well as study – **25 to napalm** (v.): here: to attack s.o. violently – **29 to lounge** (v.): /laʊndʒ/ to stand, sit or lie in a lazy relaxed way – **31 nonchalance** (n.): /ˈnɒnʃələns/ the state of being and not seeming interested in anything – **38f. to flash a look** (v.): to look quickly – **45 insuperable** (adj.): difficult or impossible to deal with – **47 histrionic** (adj.): very loud and emotional – **54 to chaperone** (v.): /ˈʃæpərəʊn/ to go somewhere with s.o. and be responsible for their behaviour – **63 surveillance** (n.): the state of being watched carefully – **67 to stump off** (v.) to walk away with heavy steps

Explanations

Intro: Friesian: coming from Friesland, a northern province of the Netherlands – **4 Perugia:** a city in central Italy, the capital of the province of Umbria – **40 femme fatale** (fr. n.): a beautiful woman who men find attractive even though she may make them unhappy – **57 *Zabriskie Point*:** released in 1970, directed by Michaelangelo Antonioni – **59f. *Ave Maria ... patate e pollo e pomodori ... santo spirito*** (it.): Hail Mary ... potatoes and chicken and tomatoes ... the Holy Spirit – **66 *Ah inglese! Va bene!*** (it.): Oh English! That's all right!

Awareness
1 What would you most like to import into Germany from other European Union countries? What do you think other countries would most want to import from Germany?

Comprehension
2 Why would being "fresh from ten years in English boarding schools" (ll. 16f.) mean that the author is "utterly unprepared for Italian womanhood" (ll. 17 ff.)?
3 Explain the effect on men indicated by the word "napalming" (l. 25).
4 What is the effect on Italian men of feminine dominance in Italian society?
5 What is, according to Henry Porter, so special about Italian women?

ANALYSIS
6 Analyse the style of Henry Porter's writing.

OPINION
7 Write a critique of the stereotypes Henry Porter presents of Italian women and British men.
8 Write an article in which you describe and make a case for something you would like to import from Britain into Germany.

PROJECT
9 Investigate attitudes towards masculinity, femininity and sexuality in Germany, Britain and Italy.

19 Britain: A Magnet for Migrants*

Britain's booming economy and the open-door policy of the present government (2006) have resulted in the largest influx of immigrants into Britain since the Second World War. Most of these immigrants have come from the new entrants to the European Union: Poland, Slovakia, the Czech Republic and the Baltic states Lithuania, Estonia and Latvia. In this article Ewa Zandman, 22, from Poland, describes her experiences as a migrant in England. – Cole Moreton, *The Independent on Sunday*, 27 August 2006, pp. 15f.

Ewa came to do a job nobody else wanted. She flew to England from Poland at the age of 22 to be a carer in a residential home, helping elderly
5 people to bathe, dress, eat and go to the toilet. The hours were long and the pay low. The work was hard, physically and mentally: she saw close up, sickness, dementia and
10 incontinence.

Ewa stuck it out. She wrestled with the language and with the loneliness, finding friends, a flat, and even love with an Englishman – for a while.
15 She made a life for herself that she likes. Ewa loves England. But now, after two years and so much effort, the way much of England seems to feel about immigrants is making
20 people like Ewa want to leave.

"If we are not wanted here, then it makes us want to go," she says quietly, speaking for herself and her sister.

The people she knows are nice, but
25 the headlines are not. The Polish are stealing jobs, living off benefits and sending the country to hell, a raging taxi driver told her. Remembering his anger with a shudder, she says: "If

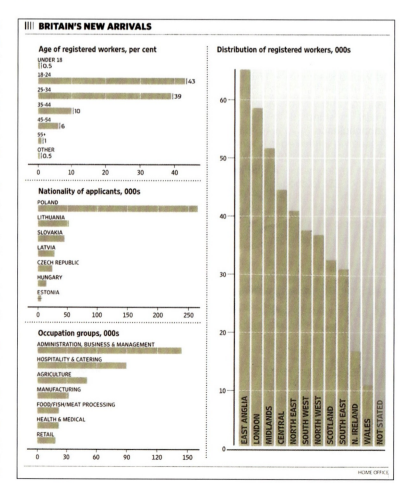

that is how people feel then maybe it is time to go to another country."

She was afraid this would happen. The first time we met, in the spring of 2004, Ewa was working as a waitress in a vegetarian restaurant in Krakow but preparing to come to England. "Is it dangerous?" she asked then, after seeing angry English people on the television ranting about the "tidal wave" of beggars, criminals and scroungers they feared would flood Britain when eight former eastern bloc countries joined the EU.

Far more people came than was expected – 600,000, it emerged last week – but only a tiny number have claimed benefits. The crime rate has not soared. Those who predicted disaster now say unemployment is being driven up and wages down. But economists and business leaders praise the new Europeans, who contribute about £2.5bn a year to the economy; and research by the Joseph Rowntree Foundation has found that employers prefer hard-working EU migrants to the British, who are perceived to be lazier and unwilling to do low-skilled work.

Ewa did not find it dangerous at all. She has made many friends here. "English people are lovely." But the angry people she saw on the television have a new scare now: the anticipated arrival of Romanians and Bulgarians in January [2007, ed.].

[...]

Now she and her sister, who is teaching here, are discussing what to do. "I do feel guilty because I know there are so many of us here and not everyone is happy with us. I worry that things will get worse."

The Zandman sisters left Poland because they could not find work – Ewa is a physiotherapist but was earning less than £100 a month in Krakow – and they do not want to go back to Poland yet. "It has so many troubles, the government is disgraceful: nationalist,

Taking care of an elderly patient

full of prejudice. So we are really thinking, if we are not wanted here, maybe we should go somewhere else?"

[...]

Ewa came with an employment agency, but hundreds of Poles continue to turn up at Victoria Coach Station every week with empty pockets and heads full of how easy it will be to get work here. Some will end up working for gangmasters on pitiful wages, paying dearly to live in hovels, or on the streets. [...]

Vocabulary

11 to stick s.th. out (v.): to continue doing s.th. that is difficult – **11 to wrestle with s.th.** (v.): /ˈresəl/ here: to try to deal with s.th. that is difficult – **26 benefits** (n. pl.): money paid by the government to people who are sick, unemployed or who have little money – **27 raging** (adj.): extremely angry – **37 to rant** (v.): to talk or complain in a loud and excited way because you feel strongly about s.th. – **38 scrounger** (n.): s.o. who tries to get money or things without doing anything for it – **51 low-skilled** (adj.): without much training or experience in a particular job – **55 scare** (n.): a situation in which a lot of people become frightened about s.th. – **75 gangmaster** (n.): s.o. who is in charge of a group of foreign workers, esp. workers who work outdoors and do not have official permission to work in Britain – **75 pitiful** (adj.): here: very low – **76 hovel** (n.): a small dirty place where s.o. lives

Explanations

25 Polish (n.): /ˈpəʊlɪʃ/ people from Poland – **34 Krakow:** also Cracow, a city with a population of 780,000 situated 300 km south of Warsaw on the River Vistula – **39 eastern bloc:** the countries of eastern and central Europe which were under Soviet domination from 1945 until the collapse of the Soviet communist system in 1989-91. – **47 bn:** short for billion (1,000,000,000) – **48 Joseph Rowntree Foundation:** one of the largest social policy research foundations in Britain. It spends about £7 million a year looking into the causes of poverty and social difficulties.

Awareness
1 Would you be prepared to go to another European country in order to work? Discuss the problems and advantages of working in another country.

Comprehension
2 Why did nobody else want the job that Ewa obtained in England?
3 What were the problems that Ewa was first confronted with in England?
4 What kind of people did some English people expect to come to England from the new EU countries in eastern and central Europe?
5 What aspects of life in Poland made Ewa come to England?

Analysis
6 Analyse Ewa's mixed feelings towards her new home.

Opinion
7 Why do you think that British employers prefer "hard-working EU migrants to the British" (ll. 49f.) and why do you think British people are unwilling to do the kind of work Ewa is doing?
8 Speculate as to why Ewa says that "English people are lovely" (l. 53).
9 Discuss the proposition that migration from the new EU members in central and eastern Europe should be stopped because these countries are losing qualified and hard-working people that they need more than Britain does.

Projects
10 Investigate and write a report on how many people and which groups of people are migrating from the new EU countries in eastern and central Europe to Britain and their effects on the British economy.
11 Find articles in the British press which try to arouse fear of migrants from the former eastern bloc countries. How are the migrants presented in them?
12 In the Internet find and consult the research compiled by the Rowntree Foundation about migrants from eastern and central Europe. Write a brief report on your findings.

20 | Nicholas Fraser
How to be a European

Most of us have, as Norman Davies wrote, 'multiple identities' (Norman Davies, *The Isles: A History*, London: Macmillan, 1999, p. xxv). They might be national and religious: German/Catholic, German/Protestant; national and regional: English/Northerner, French/Breton, German/Bavarian; bi-national within a state: British/Scottish, Spanish/Basque; and bi-national crossing state borders because of migration or marriage or both: British/German, German/Turkish, French/Spanish, depending on the origins of our parents. As European integration progresses and as international mobility increases there will be more and more of these bi-national identities. – Nicholas Fraser, *Continental Drifts: ravels in the New Europe* (London: Vintage, 1998), pp. 286–8.

Only months previously, in the summer of 1944, allied bombers had destroyed the never picturesque port of Le Havre, taking with it the spare and ugly Protestant temple. This is why my parents were married in the village churchyard of Le Hanouard, deep in the Pays de Caux. My mother had been to Britain in the 1930s as a girl; and my father was introduced to her by one of his fellow-officers, who had kept her address. I have a photograph of the occasion, which shows threadbare French attempts to keep up with the impressive chic of British Army brass. I admire my mother's and grandmother's floral dresses, and I like to look at the rogueish expression of my French grandfather, decorated veteran, failed cotton-broker, football-club manager, black-market-dealer, keeper of a POW camp, *coureur* – the word is untranslateable. And I see my tall father, for the first time in his own life truly leaving Britain and his mother.

I find in the group photograph – it must be one of so many taken that year – the attempts of Europeans to make the best of things and be happy after catastrophe. These are lucky Europeans, of course. For them the condition of liberation is real, and so, too, though they wouldn't put it that way, being pragmatic people exhausted by war, is the idea of Europe itself.

But I also tell myself that this is a private fiction of mine. These are French and British people in the photograph, and that's how they will stay. My father will return home with his French wife, and I will be born. The frontiers will go up, and something known as the Cold War will come to dominate most of my life. I will try to write about the strange hybrid quality of a 'Europe' that, outside the realm of geography or regulation, only half exists. I'll call myself 'half-French' or 'Anglo-French', aware that this is a less than satisfactory form of self-definition and wishing periodically that Europeanness could be made to mean something outside the passport queue.

It also occurs to me that autobiography European-style is a tendentious activity. Am I French or British? Does it matter? A little – to me it matters, anyhow. I suppose it ensures a double loyalty, or even a triple one: first British, or French, then European. But I sense that the third must remain problematical. What does it mean to be European? Does it mean anything at all?

There are the near-infinite Europes of memory, and these comprise our private imaginations, and there is the not-so-new 'Europe' which is neither public in the old sense, raising armies or confidently dispensing laws, nor wholly certain of what it is there to do. Somewhere between them lie the old nation-states of Europe, which are starting to look distinctly tatty, threatened in some instances by newer, less effective versions of themselves under the guise of such mysterious imperatives as regionalism or – the most confusing entity of all – federalism. These Europes coexist in each consciousness, but they have no real connection to each other. To be a European at this moment is to slide or jump uneasily from one Europe to another – they are like computer programs, which though they can be run together cannot merge.

Vocabulary

9 threadbare (adj.): (of clothes) very thin and in bad condition - **11 brass** (n.): /brɑːs/ (infml.) officers - **12 rogueish** (adj.): looking amused, esp. because you have done s.th. wrong - **14 broker** (n.): s.o. who buys and sells things - **15 POW:** also PoW, short for prisoner of war - **32 hybrid** (adj.): consisting of two or more things - **33 realm** (n.): a general area of knowledge - **40 tendentious** (adj.): expressing a strong opinion that is intended to influence poeople - **49 to dispense** (v.): here: make - **52 tatty** (adj.): (infml.) in bad condition, shabby - **54 guise** (n.): outer appearance which hides the true nature of s.th. - **55 imperative** (n.): here: s.th. that demands your urgent attention - **61 to merge** (v.): to join things together to form one thing

Explanations

1 allied (adj.): belong to the British and American air forces - **3 Le Havre:** a port in Normandy, northern France, on the mouth of the River Seine; the name means the harbour. - **4 temple:** a Protestant church built in 1862 - **5f. Pays de Caux:** departement on the Normandy coast - **15 *coureur*** (Fr. n.): literally runner; s.o. who carries out illegal trade - **31 Cold War:** the state of political conflict that existed between the Soviet bloc countries and the Western powers after the Second World War. It ended with the collapse of the communist system in 1991.

Awareness
1 What are the main elements which make up your "identity"?

Comprehension
2 Where does Nicholas Fraser's mother come from?
3 Why are the people in the photo "lucky" (l. 22)?
4 Where did Nicholas Fraser's parents live after they were married?
5 What does Nicholas Fraser mean when he writes that Europe has a "strange hybrid quality" (l. 32)?
6 What, according to Nicholas Fraser, are the problems faced by European states?
7 What do you think Nicholas Fraser means by the "near-infinite Europes of memory" (l. 46)?

Analysis
8 Sum up and explain Nicholas Fraser's complex and sometimes contradictory thoughts about Europe.

Opinion
9 Why do you think that Nicholas Fraser writes that the idea of Europe held by the people in his parents' wedding photo is only "a private fiction" (l. 26) of his?
10 In what ways do we gain from having "multiple identities" and what problems can arise from them?

Projects
11 Write a report on either someone you know or a well-known person who has parents of two different nationalities. Find out and discuss how they have coped with the linguistic and cultural challenges that they have encountered.

The flags of three countries and three regions: France (top left), Britanny (top right), Germany (middle left), Bavaria (middle right), Spain (bottom left), and the Basque Country (bottom right)